"... In Pursuit
of the
American
Dream"

"... In Pursuit of the American Dream"

BOB DOTSON

New York ATHENEUM *1985*

Library of Congress Cataloging-in-Publication Data

Dotson, Bob.
    "—In pursuit of the American dream".

    1. United States—Social life and customs—1971–
Addresses, essays, lectures. I. Title.
E169.02.D6 1985   973.92   85–47600
ISBN 0–689–11628–4

Designed by Kathleen Carey
First Edition

To
PAUL B. BAILEY,
my grandfather,
who told me to speak distinctly.

Acknowledgments

If you had asked me what my dream was when I was a boy, I would not have said, "To write a book." Writing was a struggle. It still is. My mother used to camp outside my room after Christmas and wait days for me to scribble a few thank-you notes to the relatives.

She would be proud of me for this page.

A lot of these stories first appeared on the NBC "Today" show. They were rewritten and expanded for this book each evening in the many remote motels my travels took me to. I want to thank Executive Producer Steve Friedman for his superior managerial wisdom not to call at night.

I also want to thank Jerome Wexler, Susan Beckett and Eric Stanley at NBC Enterprise for their encouragement and unwavering faith in this project; former NBC News President Reuven Frank and his successor, Lawrence Grossman, who graciously allowed these stories to appear here; and Lee Allan Smith, the General Manager of KTVY-TV (formerly WKY-TV), Oklahoma City, who did likewise.

Writing is a solitary profession. Television is not. Many talented journalists worked on these stories and helped to shape them. Their names should be on these pages too.

My special thanks to Bert Medley and Sara Pecker, to Bob Bailey, Jim Townley, Toby Weaver, Joe Torelli, Penny Fleming, Ernie Schultz, George Wesley, Oliver Murray, Jim Hulsey, Henry Kokojan, Bob Eshbaugh, Bob Brandon, Roddy Bell, Phil Lauter, Jim Watt, Houston Hall, Craig White, Jim Geraghty, Bruce Bernstein, Scotty Berner, Chuck Stewart, Darrell Barton, Chuck Fekete, Al Storey, Wolfe Fraser, Mike Tcherkassky, Randy Birch, Charlie Ray, Rob Kane, Alan Evans, Warren Jones, Frank Beacham, Corky Gibbons, Ed Johnston, Alan Stecker, and Larry Ashley.

The man who taught me to write, my first boss, is now a journalism professor at Colorado State University. Through the years, Fred Shook kept after me to complete this book. I doubted I could describe what my cameras had seen. He told me simply to "look through the picture window in your mind and tell me what's there." Fred Shook proofread what I wrote, encouraged me, and has seen it through to the end. He is my best friend.

Cathy Romine worked two jobs, seven days a week, for nearly half a year to type and retype this manuscript. She would plop down at our house each Saturday and Sunday and peck away at the computer so I could spend time with the family.

My partner and my pal, the former Linda Puckett, has been with me since the first chapter of this book. We've been married —personally and professionally—for thirteen years. That marriage is the best decision I ever made.

I have been surrounded from the beginning by people who love me, and that has made a difference.

My only daughter, Amy, who is nine, had to write a paper in school the other day describing an unfulfilled dream. She wrote about this book. That night I told her the book was finished. She started for the coatrack.

"Where're you going?"

"I wonder if it's too late to get my paper back," she said.

People still have dreams. Thanks to all of you who shared them with me.

> Bob Dotson
> January 10, 1985
> Atlanta, Georgia

Preface

Gulls pumped past us into the rising sun. Boats grumbled below. Feet shifted. The aluminum ladder shook, and a face peered down.

"You okay?"

Clutching tightly to a rung, I closed my eyes.

"Sure."

I lied.

I had pursued many an American dream for the NBC "Today" show, but this was more nightmare than dream. We were suspended twelve stories above New York harbor on a piece of thin metal ladder tilted between the pedestal and the big toe of the Statue of Liberty. Behind us the sun began to burn through a dirty ashtray sky. The morning's first boatload of tourists scurried up from the pier. We inched on.

"Give me your hand."

I looked up.

The statue's moss-colored gown was riddled with rust.

My partner in this craziness held me tightly while I threw my leg over a broken chain at the base of the statue.

"Careful. She gives underfoot."

I took a tentative step. Her copper skin was as dry as old canoes.

"Easy . . ."

I lurched around the ladder and grabbed for the statue's big toe. It was the size of a couch.

"Oh, wow! Look at all the tourists down there."

I was too busy. Hugging.

"Listen."

A sound like crickets.

We peeked over the toenail. Hundreds of people were taking pictures.

"Help me with the pole."

Bob Dotson and Peter B. Kaplan perched on Liberty's foot

He twirled a camera onto the end of a small rod and tele-scoped it seventeen feet out over the edge. A fine thread ran from the shutter button to an assistant below.

"Fire!"

CLICK.

"Oh, that's nice . . ."

Peter B. Kaplan is well known for such daredevil shots. He has taken photos atop the TV tower of the Empire State Building and suspended beneath the Brooklyn Bridge. Now, the National Park Service was allowing him to go where no other photographer had gone before. He had hung from Liberty's torch; shot from the tablet tucked in her arms; crawled over the crown. His pictures of her many moods taken from remarkable positions will be used to raise money for the statue's restoration.

"I've been injured only once," he smiled, scuttling back from the edge, "in a fall from a folding chair, taking wedding pictures."

But this assignment would be his most difficult.

"When I go into the torch," he said, settling onto the toe, "sometimes it can be cruel as h__. The arm sways seven feet in the wind. Going up hand over hand, the wind shifts and the whole arm goes BONG! I've almost lost my fingers from the cold up there." He brought the camera to his eye. "But the view, oh, that view, is beautiful."

You could fill an ocean liner with the number of people who take the statue's picture each day. It is a vision of America over-laid many times. Yet, Peter B. Kaplan is looking for what has not been seen.

"We're sitting here on her toe," he said, stroking the statue's ankle. "Who would ever dream we'd be sitting on the statue's toes? I feel I'm a part of her almost."

Our eyes lingered on the New York skyline.

"Most people call this place a jungle," he said softly. "I call it a jungle gym."

Kaplan dipped around Liberty's dress. The folds had holes large enough to take pictures through. He did so. Where he stood, rivets were rotting out. The wind and salt and time had taken their toll.

"I don't know how she's survived," he sighed.

The statue has lasted because a young French engineer figured a way to hang each copper section independently so none would weigh on its neighbor. The young man was so successful, folks in Paris asked him to build a tower for them.

Mr. Eiffel said he would.

Liberty was a gift to America from Frédéric Auguste Bartholdi. He fashioned the statue's face in the image of his mother. The arms were molded after his wife's, and he found the soul of us all.

Liberty's light rose just as America opened wide its shores. The nickels and dimes of a million immigrants put her in place. Eight out of ten of us today have ancestors who first saw America beneath Liberty's torch. They journeyed a troubled road, dreading the darkness. They passed a gentle mother who held up hope.

Not every immigrant found success, but the wilderness beyond that torch was part of their geography of hope. Thirty-six thousand sunsets have colored New York harbor in the century since the statue was built, yet she still stands—a kind of national conscience—welcoming, sheltering. The Statue of Liberty has become an enduring monument to what could be and what is right.

"I think these broken chains attracted me to the statue more than anything else," said Kaplan, stepping over the shattered shackles at the statue's feet. "Liberty tramping over tyranny."

He started down the ladder.

"I thought I might get bored. She's so familiar, but I just watch the people. They never stop coming."

I am the luckiest of television network news correspondents. My beat takes me in pursuit of the American dream. It is not the usual pursuit of love or money or fame; it is a chronicle of our people and how we struggle to build, discover, create, achieve, survive, and grow.

In the past fifteen years, I have crisscrossed the country—first for WKY-TV (now KTVY-TV) in Oklahoma City, then for the NBC "Today" show, now for NBC "Nightly News with Tom Brokaw"—seeking the kinds of people who might live next door or just down the street. My job is to find the extraordinary in ordinary lives; to look for the common threads that link a lonely sheepherder in Nevada to a group of young poets on a forgotten island off the coast of Georgia. I work the neglected corners of our cities. The small towns. The dirt roads. I look for these stories because I believe they tell us something of the larger issues that we all face day by day.

Too often in television news, reporters content themselves with showing politicians getting on and off airplanes. Not much we do reflects how people actually live. Back in the 1930s, the government sent great numbers of out-of-work filmmakers, writers, and photographers to comb the countryside and record the common activities of life. The effort of that remarkable band of journalists is now a benchmark by which we measure that time. Their work has proved to be of immeasurable importance long after film clips of politicians stepping on and off railroad cars have crumbled in neglect.

I like the idea that we can see a bit of ourselves in these reports; that all our lives and our dreams are important and really matter. After all, this country was built not by great heroes or great politicians, but by ordinary people—by thousands whose names we don't know, may never know, but without whose influence America wouldn't exist.

Television is at its best when it shows people to people, for such stories mirror our lives and our heritage and help us to understand ourselves better. You will find that it makes little difference where the folks on these pages live or what they do. What is important is who they are. They are music for the mind, each with his own voice, to sing us a chorus of our times.

Contents

Contents

Contents

xix

ONE

No Matter How Bad Things Get, People Can Survive

"*. . . I done a little bit of everything
to make a living for my kids.*"
FLORENCE THOMPSON

The Mona Lisa
of the Thirties

MODESTO, CALIFORNIA
(1979)

For most of the families who lived in the 1930s Dust Bowl, *depression* was not an abstract economic term. Their farms were buried in burned-out soil, and with nowhere to turn, they moved on. They went the way Americans have always gone for new beginnings—to the West. In a fifteen-month period, eighty-six thousand desperate people crossed into California, more than twice the number who went looking for gold in 1849. Along the way, they liked to talk about how things would be when they bought their little white homes in the orange groves. It was a dream they all carried, but a dream that blew away like the dust they had fled.

Instead of new homes, they found migrant camps and two or three hungry families for each job; so they learned to live where there was no work, and through hope and daring, they learned to survive. All this seems like shopworn history, but its lesson is that these people never lost sight of what they could achieve.

They followed the dream no matter where it blew, and they made life better.

Today there is a trailer camp on the site of the old migrant camp in Modesto, California. Many of the people who live here now, lived here then. During the Depression, it was just one of many stops on their endless road. Now it is home. Here we found Florence Thompson, the Mona Lisa of the 1930s, a migrant mother whose picture haunted the nation. Florence Thompson. No, you wouldn't recognize the name, but few could forget her face.

Florence Thompson was twenty-seven years old when the

"Migrant Mother" photographed by Dorothea Lange

4

Depression started. She had five children and was pregnant with another—and her husband had died.

"I chopped cotton for forty cents an acre in them days," said Florence. She was sitting with some friends just inside the door to her little blue trailer. You could see her carefully tended flower garden from where she sat. There was no copy of her famous picture on the wall. Looking at her now, it was difficult to find a trace of that younger woman in her face. "I used to fill up those old cotton sacks 'til I couldn't even lift them," she said. "Worked before daylight 'til it got so dark I couldn't see. And I didn't even weigh a hundred pounds."

The others in the room—two neighbors and a visiting relative—nodded their heads in understanding. They were all about Florence's age. Outside, a man with a cane stopped to admire her flowers and called out a greeting. She went to the screen door and waved, then turned back to her chair. Her face was deeply lined.

Florence Thompson today

"I had to drag those hundred pound sacks of cotton," she continued. "The scales were halfway across the field." Her voice dropped to a whisper. She looked out at her flowers. The sun from the open door fell upon her face. Florence shifted in her seat.

"I'd pick five hundred pounds each day," she whispered.

The room was quiet. Down the road somewhere, we could hear a domino game, then the neighborhood dogs began to bark, and there was a knock at the door. Behind the screen were two middle-aged women, Florence Thompson's daughters, Ruby and Catherine. They had come to take their mother to a family reunion. Catherine works in a turkey factory; Ruby raises pigeons for the gourmet table. They both make more in one hour than their mother used to make in a week.

"If she could have gave us all material things, maybe she would have," said Ruby after introductions had been made, "but I don't think that would replace what she did give us." Ruby looked at her mother, who now stood before a mirror, fixing her hair. "She gave us a sense of worth and the belief that nobody owes us anything!"

They did not have much, but they had each other. Florence Thompson kept the family together. Her ten children and their grandchildren still live in her valley, and they still gather each year in memory of a father some of them never knew.

"Watch the birdie," called a photographer at the reunion later that afternoon. It was a clear, warm, fall day, and the family was picnicking in a park. Moments before, a dozen kids had scampered to the swings while their mothers begged them to stay clean. It was time for the family portrait. No time for mud.

"Move in a little closer," said the photographer. He slipped a black plate into the back of his camera, as relatives—ten rows deep—tried to wedge themselves between swingsets and seesaws. The smaller children squirmed. Their parents pinched them into place.

"Smile!"

6

Ruby and Catherine squinted into the sun. Florence was not with them. She had stayed home. At the last minute, she had decided not to go. She would not say why. Alone in her kitchen, she finally looked at a copy of her famous picture.

"I don't think you could take a woman today and put her out and do what I done to make a living," she said. She ran her fingers across the old photo as if to clean the dust from the tired face that stared back. "I worked in hospitals. I tended bar. I cooked. I worked in the field. I done a little bit of everything to make a living for my kids."

Beyond her screen door, the bees and the hummingbirds were at work in her garden. Florence Thompson watched them for a moment, then set the picture aside and stepped outside.

"Did you ever lose hope?" I asked.

"Nope," she said, snapping off a flower and lifting it to smell. "If I'd a lost hope, we never would have made it."

Shadow and Light

The Great Depression of the 1930s did not begin with the stock market crash or the closing of banks. It began with dust. Dust that swept from a hundred million acres and swirled off the plains like a coffee-colored blizzard that killed cattle and covered crops. In one day, three hundred fifty million tons of topsoil were sucked into the sky, carried aloft on one-hundred-mile-an-hour winds. Twelve million tons of dirt fell on Chicago. The rest soared on toward the Atlantic. Ships three hundred miles from New York reported dust on their decks.

In the West, there was drought. In the East, there were floods. One hundred thousand people fought the Mississippi River during the summer of 1937, but the water backed into Arkansas, Tennessee, Illinois, and Missouri. Farms were ruined. Houses were torn loose. Nearly one million people floated from their land.

Cotton prices in Arkansas dropped to gut level. In Cimarron County, Oklahoma, where the worst dust storms hit, there was a year when not a blade of wheat was harvested. The blowing dirt and the floods were so bad that by mid-Depression two million farmers were out of work. And for most, the future held only a mirror on the times.

The federal government resettled some families in model communities built on productive farms. Each man was given forty acres and a mule and five years to work his way out of poverty. Most of the resettlements withered away when World War II brought jobs and better times, but Lake View, Arkansas, survived. More than half the families who moved there eventually bought their own land and stayed. They had come from generations of sharecroppers who had never owned their own farms. For them, land was a way out of poverty. They would not give it up.

Jones Phillips moved to Lake View in 1938. He and his brother, Leon, had come to look for a better life. They never doubted they had found it here.

"What's the price of these eggs?" said Jones, tapping a carton on the grocer's shelf. He is a small man and this is a small store, an old-fashioned place with a cooler of hot soda pop and pork sticks floating in a glass jar near the cash register. The building is made of wood and resembles a matchbox. It sits at the side of Main Street, overlooking the lake that gave the town its name. Jones had brought us here to make a point.

"How much'd ya say these were?" said Jones, waving the carton over his head. His eyes were on his visitors.

"A dollar and ten cents," replied the grocer. It was apparent that the grocer had been through this drill before.

"A dollar and ten cents!" echoed Jones in a voice two times his size. His eyes swept the store, counting his audience. Two kids over by the candy jars were more interested in Jujubes.

"Used to be I'd have to get them eggs on credit," said Jones. "Maybe it would take me a month to pay for them."

The grocer sighed. Jones waved his free hand with a flourish and thrust it into his overalls.

"Today I can reach into my pocket and pay for them now!"

The kids poured two handfuls of candy on the checkout counter.

"That'll be a dollar sixty," said the grocer.

Ten years after the Depression, Jones Phillips was out of debt. He and his wife, Lou Gussie, raised ten children and had sixty-nine grandchildren. All of them finished high school, and half went to college. One of Leon's ten children, Leon, Jr., is superintendent of schools in Lake View. He is also city recorder, and in his spare time farms his dad's original forty acres.

"I wanted to succeed so badly," said Jones.

Leon (left) and Jones Phillips as young men

Jones Phillips displays his eggs

We were sitting at a picnic table at Lake View Park. The sun was low over the water. Fishermen in wooden boats floated slowly between the cypress stumps in front of us. Their rhythmic casting was back lit, turning nylon fishing lines silver in the sun. We watched the lines crisscross among the trees, weaving giant cobwebs.

"I just wanted something of my own," Jones repeated. He had said it once before, but I had been daydreaming. I turned away from the fishermen. "I wanted something for my children," he said and held my eyes. Jones's face was filled with conviction. His words took on real meaning. "I wanted to send them out in the world for themselves so they would do a better job than we did."

Darrell Coble was three years old when the stinging sand sent him scurrying with his father and brother to the shelter of a half-hidden barn. They lived in Cimarron County at the very tip of the Oklahoma panhandle—in the deepest pocket of the dust.

"See those old trees sitting down yonder?" he said, pointing into the distance. His children scuttled up behind him, scattering yellow flowers underfoot, and looked where he pointed. "Them

A young Darrell Coble approaches the barn with his father and brother

are locust trees." Darrell took off his straw hat and wiped a line of sweat from his forehead. "There was only about two foot of 'em sticking out of the grit when I was your age."

Coble has brought his children on this warm October day to see the old homestead. The trees and the house still stand as monuments to those dusty times.

"Let's look inside!" yelled the boy.

"Be careful, now," said Darrell.

His kids don't remember when more than half the neighbors left, blown-out, baked-out, broke. By Depression's end, there were fewer than two people per square mile in Cimarron County. The Cobles still live less than twelve miles from the original home. Despite the dust and the drought, Darrell's dad stuck it out.

"They tried to get him to go to California," said Darrell, as he watched his boy and girl pry a large iron patch from the door. "Dad said, 'No way.'" Darrell paused as his kids squealed and slid inside.

He and the stranger now stood alone. Coble propped his elbow on a fence post and rested his boot on the bottom strand of barbed wire. He took out a cigarette and surveyed the old house in silence. Its roof sagged in the middle like a swaybacked horse. The porch was gone. A bedroom had only three sides still standing. Faded wallpaper flapped in the wind.

Coble looked beyond to the corral and watched the tumbleweed curl around the fence posts. He was a slight man, dressed in jeans and a work shirt, with a face that could sell Marlboros. He listened to the sound of crickets mix with his children's laughter from behind the door, then lowered his boot to the ground.

The old homestead as it looks today

"Dad told me he'd rather stay in the dust than go out to California on someone else's money."

Much has been written about the Okies who left their farms and headed west, but little about those who remained—those who rebuilt the land, renewed the soil, and ended the Dust Bowl. When the rains returned in 1941, Darrell and his neighbors dug dozens of man-made lakes and changed the way they plowed to lock the topsoil in place.

His father, Arthur Coble, had come to Cimarron County from Illinois in 1916, determined to buy his own farm. The Depression forced him to rent almost all of his life. Darrell worked a second job for twelve years to keep his dad's dream alive. They now own some of the land they till, but it took thirty-seven years to raise the down payment.

"Some of my older boys are worried that this inflation and recession may take our farm," said Darrell Coble as he turned for a last look at the old homestead. "But if bad times come, I figure they can find some comfort in this place."

Today in Lake View, Arkansas, as in so many small towns, the streets are paved with memories, not dreams. The alleys echo what used to be. Machines have long since replaced stooped shoulders and aching backs out in the cotton fields, and the offer of forty acres and a mule, which had helped Jones Phillips lift himself from poverty, is now gone. Those who did not get government help in the 1930s have little hope of owning land today.

"There ain't no use in me trying," said Geneva Euing, who lives down the dirt road from the park in Lake View. Her children were playing Frisbee in the front yard. She was sitting outside on the cinder block steps that led to her living room. "All I can do is pay for this home, if I can."

She sighed. "I got thirty-two years to go."

"Catch it, Mama!" yelled one of the boys as the Frisbee sailed up near the steps. Geneva lunged, but missed, then straightened herself. She is a young woman, tired beyond her years.

"Don't know where I'll be in thirty-two years," she said.

"Come on, kids, time to go!" shouted Darrell.

There were giggles behind the door. Coble tilted his hat back and picked at an old feed calendar that was stuck up on a wall. The children popped out from under the iron patch.

"Look, Pa!" laughed the girl. "A recipe book."

"And it's only got two pages," said the boy.

"Didn't eat a whole lot back then," Darrell grinned. "Come on, Mother'll be waiting supper on us."

The three walked off in single file across the field and left the old homestead to the wind.

"Gimme that old time religion.
Gimme that old time religion.
Gimme that old time religion.
It's good enough for me. . . ."

It is Sunday morning and the music pours forth from a building that has no foundation. It is a wooden church, painted white, that rests on cinder blocks. The floor is several feet off the ground and bounces with the stomping of one hundred feet. Inside, in the front row, little girls in starched dresses sit with their mothers and grandmothers.

Beneath an open window, Jones Phillips said simply, "Lake View will endure." He is a man who molded the Depression into a better life. He believes that today's problems can also be solved. He still has faith that the future can correct the past.

"This town is filled with born-again people," he said with certainty in his voice.

Through the
Looking Glass, Darkly

For nearly a century Oklahoma was primarily a land of the red and the black, a checkerboard of Indians and ex-slaves, who very nearly got their own state. As America pushed West, 110 tribes found refuge there. It was Indian territory then, but some of the chiefs were black men.

I stumbled upon this extraordinary tale while looking for Charlie Ellison, who I'd been told was the last man in these parts who could sing the ancient sacred harp spirituals, hymns that date back to slave days and are sung unaccompanied.

I found him sitting alone in a field of daisies, his legs splayed out in front of him, a tattered hymnal spread open on his knees. He looked to be past ninety. It was a brilliant, warm spring day. His head was back, eyes tightly shut. Charlie Ellison was soaking up some sun.

He seemed rather formally dressed for a field full of daisies. He had on a sports coat. His chin covered his tie, and his collar points soared upward. Ellison had the kind of neck that fights buttons.

There was an old weathered church on the hillside behind him. He wanted to try his song there.

> "There is a melancholy place
> for those who have no God . . ."

The voice was clear, deep and perfectly pitched, but it trailed away. His finger was shaking on the page.

"I can't sing it by myself, hardly," said Ellison softly. Crickets picked up the chorus.

Charlie Ellison was a black man but looked curiously like an Indian. I asked him about that. He admitted he was one of the first Americans, but said we had never seen the looking glass of his mind. His history had always been there, but we had never looked through the looking glass, darkly.

Then he led me to a handful of friends, who told me a tale seldom told.

"When Andrew Jackson had all the Indians on the Trail of Tears, whether the history books show it or not, a great percentage of those people were black people."

Percy Alexander's voice was full of memory. He was a farmer about Ellison's age. He paused in his work and leaned against a fence.

"A lot of the colored, you see, ran off from the plantations, and them Indians, they harbored them in. All up and down the Mississippi River was just a dark swamp. And they could never get them colored folks out of there. They stayed in there."

Alexander pulled on his hoe.

"Them Indians had the awfulest time. I heard my mother and them talking about it. I was a boy about seven or eight years old. They would beat 'em. They shot 'em. They'd kill 'em. They just murdered 'em all kinds of ways, and run 'em on back across the Mississippi River. Back over into Oklahoma. This place wasn't fitten for nothing else, so the United States gov'ment just decided to let 'em have this place. Give 'em this and never bother 'em about it anymore.

"The Trail of Tears treaty said as long as the oak and ash would grow, as long as the water'd run downstream, they'd never be bothered about this country."

No one knows for certain how many blacks came to Oklahoma on the Trail of Tears. Census takers in those days didn't bother to knock on doors, and runaway slaves weren't answering any roll calls.

"Slaves would go back, slip out at night, and go back to old Marsters' and them's farms. Kill a hog and cut it all up. On the way home, they'd start a song."

Alexander beat time on his hoe.

> " 'Way back, 'way back . . .
> I'm going to my shanty, 'way back.
> The houn' dog's on my track
> And the chicken's on my back,
> But I'm goin' to make it to my shanty,
> 'Way back . . .''

His old eyes strayed across the meadow to focus on the sound of chickens somewhere in the distance.

"The slaves would get turpentine and put it all under the bottom of their feet to keep the dogs from trackin' 'em. The property owners would come out with the hounds and go and run 'em in the woods. Probably catch a whole lot of 'em. Every time they caught a slave, they got seven hundred dollars for that slave. That's the way they made their living."

Not all of the runaways found freedom among the Indians. Some of the tribes in the South had plantations of their own. A black back was the going thing in a cotton field, no matter what color the field's owner happened to be.

"All of them Indians from Northern Georgia, Tennessee, and all, when they were moved out West, they carried their slaves with them."

Antoine Fuhr picked up the story. He was dapperly dressed, sitting under a honeysuckle bush with two friends, Jim Simmons, a successful rancher, and the Reverend Charles Davis. The three had just come from a funeral. All were in their eighties. All had faces you might find on an Indian-head nickel.

"The slaves were the ones that taught the Indians agriculture, house building, and how to make a living, other than fishing and hunting. Because that was the Indian's tradition, this fishing and hunting. That's the reason why these eastern Indians got to be known as the five 'Civilized Tribes.' Them people lived like civilized people.

"Some of the blacks, of course, married into the Indian families. That's why there were so many black Indians, Creek and Seminole Indians."

David Wisener held an aging picture of himself. A small black boy wearing buckskin, furs, and feathers stared back. Wisener, a deacon, was the same age as the others. He paused, pursed his lips, and examined the photograph. Antoine Fuhr continued.

"Many of the Indians that ranked way high were black people. Most people don't know that Osceola, the chief of the Seminoles, was half Negro. His mother was a Negro woman. But his father was a chief.

"Look at Jim Simmons over there if you want to. He's about two-thirds Indian. But on the tribal rolls, he's a black man all right. Look at Reverend Davis. He's about a quarter-breed. But the rolls say he's a Negro."

19

David Wisener as a boy

Wisener passed his picture around, then said, "Bud and Ed Cox were well-known Creek Indian citizens, black freedmen. They operated a big ranch out there five miles west of Wetumka. Every summer they would have a branding festival. They'd get out and round up the cattle. Maybe a thousand or fifteen hundred head of them at a time.

"All the ranching business was done by colored. All the Oklahoma cowboys were colored. The Indians and the colored owned all the land."

Few of the men who rode after cattle kept accurate journals. As a rule, they wrote history with their horses and punctuated it with their six-guns. And yet, with passing references to "Black Sam" or simply to "a colored man named Charlie," it is clear that no fewer than three thousand black cowboys passed through Oklahoma. One of them originated the most popular event in rodeo.

Clarence Christian added this memory to the field of daisies.

"Speaking of Mr. Pickett, Bill Pickett, I knew him not intimately, but I knew him real well. He was grown and I was a child. It just so happened that as kids'll do, I kinda caught myself a little sweet on his granddaughter. This enabled me to be around him quite a while.

"Mr. Pickett had some livestock on a little acreage he was working. Occasionally they'd get out and that would kinda irritate him. He would have to hunt 'em down at night, and the neighbors'd squawk. One day, one of his cows got out. His wife called him, told him that the cow was gone, and he'd have to hunt for it."

Christian grinned like a man with a secret.

"Mr. Pickett wasn't too good with a rope. He could ride real well, better than average, but his roping left something to be desired."

He stopped to let that sink in.

"Well, he chased that cow, and he couldn't get a rope on him. Seemingly, through a fit of anger, he decided just to manhandle this cow.

"He rode alongside of him. He got off on him. He leaned over between his horns and bit the cow on the nose.

"This threw the cow off balance. The cow stumbled. Mr. Pickett just held on with his teeth and fell on over his head.

"When he hit the ground, this sudden jerk threw the cow. To his amazement—he wanted to know if it was just a freak thing or whether it was something out of the ordinary—he tried it again. And it worked again.

"So according to him, and his daughter, Miss Nellie, that's how the rodeo sport of bulldogging was really originated."

Congress gave black men the unpopular task of keeping the peace in Indian territory. During the Civil War, troops were removed from the western edge of Oklahoma, and Plains Indians began to raid the herds of the Chickasaws and Choctaws, two of the "Civilized Tribes" to the east. Bootleggers and horse thieves entered illegally, and encroaching white settlements threatened to set Oklahoma onto a war path.

Six black army regiments were formed and sent West. Two were to be stationed in Oklahoma. General George Armstrong Custer was asked to command one of them, but he refused, and in so doing set his path to the Little Big Horn ten years later.

Officially, those who patrolled the Oklahoma border were known as the Ninth and Tenth Cavalries. But to those who knew them best—the Cheyennes, Comanches, and Kiowas—they will always be remembered as the Buffalo Soldiers.

To the Indian, the black man's nappy hair resembled buffalo hide. And the name, a mixture of fear and respect, stuck. For twenty tempestuous years, the Buffalo Soldiers protected Indians from Indians, and whites from renegades, and themselves from both. They fought in every major Indian war in the Southwest. They quieted the frontier, and in the process, won twelve Congressional Medals of Honor.

The Reverend Charles Davis hoisted his cane for attention.
"Bass Reeves!"
We looked at one another for some clue as to what was to come. The only sound was a disinterested bee in a honeysuckle bush.
"I can tell you more about him than perhaps you ever heard."
Davis waited dramatically, then proceeded in a big, booming voice.

"The laws were written by the Indian and Negro legislation. The officers of the law, the chief ones among us in Indian territory, were known as U.S. marshals. They came in from the States. They were paid by the United States government.

"Bass Reeves came from Arkansas as one of those United States marshals. Bass was a kind, sympathetic man, but he was a brave man, mentally and physically strong. He could whip most any two men with his fists. He was a man that when he went after a group, now, brother, he'd bring you in. But he was kind and sympathetic. He never booted in and caused trouble.

"I have seen him come into a community and come to a church on Sunday and have a warrant for somebody. Call him out and say, 'I've got a warrant for you. Would you mind coming into Muskogee to the marshal's office tomorrow morning?' He'd say that nicely. 'I don't know what it is, but you'd better go see about it. If I have to arrest you, you see, they'll have to take you to Fort Smith, and you'll be away from your family and everything.' And he got lots of his work done just that way.

"His son grew up here. He married one of the native women and, something or another, they got into trouble. He killed her. He murdered her. Leo Bennett was the head marshal. He was arming his men. He got word that the boy was determined not to be arrested alive, threatened them not to come to his house because he wasn't going to be arrested.

"Bass got ahold of it. Bass went to the office, Leo Bennett's office, and asked them not to go up there.

" 'Some of you will get killed. Let me have the warrant, and I'll go up there. It is a bench warrant. I'll do just what the warrant says. I'm going to bring him in dead or alive.'

"That's right. Well, the people knew he would. A number of them followed him to the house where the young man was, begging him, insisting that he not do it, for fear he might get killed. But he went on about his business, got to the house and yelled to this boy. His name was Benny.

" 'Now, Benny,' he said. 'You're no more my son.' That's right. 'You committed a crime, and I have a warrant in my pocket for you, a bench warrant. It's either to bring you in dead or alive. I'm going to take you in today one way or the other. That's all there is to it. You can come out with your hands up or else your whole body will be down.' "

Davis rubbed his cane handle, relishing the moment.

"Benny came out."

He paused.

"The people standing around hollered to him, 'Don't raise your hands because he'll kill you sure. Bass was sent to get you, and he means to do it.' "

Davis slowly lifted his cane and aimed it like a rifle. The cane spent more time in the air, emphasizing his words than it did on the ground. After a while, he dropped it.

"They arrested Benny and took him in. Benny went to the penitentiary.

"You see, to commit a crime was something awful, and whoever did it, he wouldn't like it, because it would be remembered forever. They would announce it all around that they was going to whip a certain man on a certain day for committing an offense. The people would come from far and near.

"There wasn't no certain whip to be beaten with. The officer'd go to the nearest woods and cut down a limb. Trim it up nicely. Bring in two or three of them for the whipping that day.

"If a fellow was caught again, it was a hundred lashes on the same back by two officers. That's right. One, fifty lashes, and the other one, fifty lashes. One man would count so there wouldn't be any missed or give too many.

"Well, now the third offense was death. That person would suffer death. There was no bond, no reprieve, no renewal of the case or nothin' of the kind. He was 'shot at sunrise,' that's what my old stepdaddy would say.

" 'You've had your trial, you've had your witnesses. The jurors have found you guilty beyond a reasonable doubt. I set your execution at sunrise next Thursday morning. That settles it.'

"They had no chamber of death. They didn't hang by rope. They had a block set up. They would set the prisoner there, tie a white cloth across his chest about where his heart was. Two officers would take a rifle and step off according to the presiding officer. Thirty feet or thirty yards. Something like that. And then turn at his command."

Davis demonstrated with his cane.

"I've seen that right at the old Lee Courthouse."

There was growing public pressure to open new homesteads in the West, and this threatened Indian territory. Americans who saw the frontier closing felt their dreams of free land slip away. Many who had no property were convinced that the "Civilized Tribes" held more than they needed.

Indian territory belonged to the tribes as a whole. The government set up the Dawes Commission in the late 1800s to assign Indian land to individuals, in hopes that some would sell to white settlers. Some did.

The commission was instructed to prepare a list of the members of each tribe. This roll was to include the Indian's ex-slaves, the black freedmen. Not all of the blacks got an even shake, but Creek freedmen got more than anybody else because of the twinkling eye of Judge Reed.

"Judge Reed was an honorable man, but he was a black man. He interpreted for all the chiefs."

Antoine Fuhr allowed as how he had never publicly told what he was about to tell, because Judge Reed had been a prominent man, and there was no percentage in embarrassing prominent men. But the judge was long past that now. He was dead.

"When they got to the allotment of the land, and the chiefs sat down with the Dawes Commission, the commission said, 'Now, we can give each Indian a hundred and sixty acres.' At

Judge Reed

least, that was what Judge Reed interpreted to the chiefs. 'Indians all get a hundred and sixty acres.'

"Well, they asked what the Indians were going to do about those black people in their tribes. 'What do they get? Don't they get something?' And the chiefs said, 'Nothing. Give them nothing.' The Dawes Commission asked Judge Reed, 'Now what did they say?' Judge Reed said, 'Chiefs say, give 'em the same thing.'

"The commission depended on his interpretation!"

Fuhr laughed with glee.

"That's how our folks got homesteads in Oklahoma."

The Reverend Davis chuckled, brushed the sleeve of his rumpled blue suit, and tapped his black round-toed shoes with his cane. When the laughter died down, he noted:

"I grew up on the through-road going West. Some of the pioneers would camp overnight, and I'd hear my mother talking with the womenfolks. They said they were on their way to the promised land. I didn't know what that meant."

He smiled.

"They were going to homestead the original Oklahoma."

The Reverend Paul Sykes was one of those who led people to the promised land. He had rolled into Kingfisher, Oklahoma, with six hundred ex-slaves the year before lands to the west were opened. To feed his people, he preached at the Rock Island railroad station. He did that for years.

Sidney Cline Church watched Paul Sykes many times from his room with a view of the railroad platform. Church was a lanky, thin Welshman who had jumped ship in Galveston, Texas,

The Reverend Paul Sykes

before World War I, hitchhiked to Oklahoma, and decided to stay.

"The old gentlemen would come down here and meet the trains. There would probably be three or four trains a day. He had his cane, and he was stooped a little bit. He would start to sing like this."

Church stood, leaned over, and began to bob up and down. He was now about the same age as he remembers the Reverend Sykes.

"Ol' ark's a-movin', a-movin', a-movin',
The ol' ark's a-movin', a-movin' right along,
Goin' up to heaven, like a feather in the air.
Ol' ark's a-movin', a-movin', a-movin',
The ol' ark's a-movin', a-movin' right along."

"That was it. That was part of his preaching, in a way of speaking. After the train had stopped, people then, of course, would throw a little money out to him. Sometimes maybe they'd throw a dollar, fifty cents. Sometimes silver dollars in those days, but mostly it was probably nickels and dimes."

Paul Sykes kept a lot of people alive that first long winter with the money he collected at the train station. Traveling salesmen also dropped off hogs and turkeys. One or two gave him a cow. Indians, blacks—and whites—came to the feasts he set out.

The Reverend Sykes continued to preach on the Rock Island railroad station platform, and for many years thereafter, he would feed two or three hundred people, three times a month. He became so well known that the railroad wanted to set him up in Chicago, but he declined. Kingfisher was his church. He never missed a train.

There is a postscript to this story from Sidney Cline Church. "In World War I the boys all left here and enlisted in the old

Oklahoma National Guard. I signed up, too. We finally got overseas. We ran into the lines. We lost a lot of good boys. I got knocked out pretty bad.

"Now I'm on the platform in Paris, France, and I'm waiting for the train to go to Le Havre to cross the English Channel to go home.

"A Frenchman asked me what part of Oklahoma was I from, and I said, 'Kingfisher.' And he studied a second, and his brows knitted.

" 'Ah,' he said. 'The black man, he dance, he sing.'

"I looked at him in amazement, and I said, 'Yes . . .'

"Well, this fellow's father had been one of those salesmen who passed through Kingfisher.

> 'Ol' ark's a-movin', a-movin', a-movin',
> The ol' ark's a-movin', a-movin' right along,
> Goin' up to heaven, like a feather in the air.
> Ol' ark's a-movin', a-movin', a-movin',
> The ol' ark's a-movin', a-movin' right along.'

"The Reverend Sykes had other songs, too, but I don't remember any of those. But I do remember that real well."

"In 1892, when I first came here, there was two frame buildings, and the rest was tents and dugouts."

Logan Jackson, a retired carpenter, spliced his thoughts with laughter. He wanted no one to think he was complaining.

"Those that had horses and cattle, they made it. But, you take a person like me, come here with nothing, just his bare hands, well, he had to dig things out for himself."

Oklahoma was one of the few places where blacks actually owned land. And from the beginning, this fact was not lost to blacks or whites. It was a seed of power and contention.

For years, a move had been under way to make Oklahoma an

all-black state. In 1890, it was spurred on by Edwin McCabe, a black man who sought appointment as territorial governor. McCabe had been state auditor of Kansas, but when his party refused to let him run for a second term, he came to Oklahoma, convinced that power lay only in numbers. For ten years, McCabe's newspaper, the *Langston Herald*, was distributed throughout the South, urging settlement in Oklahoma's all-black towns.

"There was between fifteen and twenty Negro towns within a fifty-mile radius of Muskogee."

Antoine Fuhr drew a circle with his hand.

"Absolute Negro towns. These colored folks, they'd hear about that. Some of them would come to see.

"There was a Negro postmaster. They'd take them on down and introduce him.

"There was a Negro mayor. Yeah, 'Call a meetin!'

"There was a Negro councilman.

"A Negro marshal, town marshal.

"Black folks come here to Muskogee, they couldn't hold one of those offices. They couldn't even get to be dogcatcher!"

The leaves crackled. Jim Simmons rocked forward in his chair.

"I remember the first white man I ever saw. His name was Ed Hodd. He gave me a dime and gave George Drew a nickel. Well, I looked at the size of the money and said, 'Now, here, I'm getting the short end of this thing.' So I just traded with George. Traded my dime for his nickel."

He boomed out a big, hearty laugh.

"I didn't know any better till we spent it for some candy. See, I didn't get but five or six sticks, and George got ten."

Antoine Fuhr was tickled.

"That was the first white man you ever saw?"

Simmons smiled broadly.

"Yes, that was the first white man. His name was Ed Hodd."

Davis nodded.

"Foreman on the Seavers Ranch."

Simmons turned to him.

"Yes, foreman on the Seavers Ranch."

Davis tapped his cane.

"That's right, I knew him."

Simmons sat back and slapped the arm of his chair.

"The first deal I made, I got stumped!"

The old men shook with laughter.

Several women joined our little band beneath the honeysuckle bush. Mrs. Andrew Rusworm ran a funeral parlor. Mrs. Blance [*sic*] Harper was twisting the lilac-colored chain that held her glasses and recalling happier times growing up out in the country.

"We'd play together. We'd run. Go over to the white girl's house. Spend the night. She'd come stay all night with us. We didn't think no more about it. We'd visit back and forth as though we were all one."

Segregation was not widespread on the farm. People needed each other. Pigment made no difference in the dust at baling time.

Mrs. Rusworm remembered.

"If one wasn't busy and another was fixing a fence, he'd come over and help him. And when his fence needed fixin', Dad would go over there and do the same."

But black homesteaders were soon outnumbered. G. I. Currin, the only black official in Oklahoma territory, lasted one term. He proposed the first civil rights bill. It did not pass.

"You couldn't vote unless your grandfather voted in eighteen and sixty-six."

Birdie Farmer, a retired schoolteacher, was nearly one hundred, a quarter of a century older than the state where she lived.

"Of course, that prohibited all Negroes from voting because no Negroes' grandparents voted in sixty-six."

Strips of deep lavender began to appear on the edge of the sky. The first feathered shadows fell on the daisies. Approaching darkness stirred Logan Jackson's memory anew.

"Dan Porter was an old Civil War veteran. I was a little boy. At the time we met, they were enforcing the Jim Crow law, which said black men couldn't vote.

"Man told Dan Porter, says, 'Don't you go in there and try to vote.' Says, 'You can't read.'

"Porter says, 'That don't make no difference. I'm one of the men who made General Lee surrender!' You don't know who General Lee was, do you?"

The old man stared into the faces around him.

"He was a general in the Civil War. Yeah, an old soldier."

"Well, Old Dan, he voted."

Oklahoma's statehood in 1907 brought new laws. Overnight, black men were told where to sit, where to walk, and when to learn.

For those who had come West with the frontier spirit, it was a bitter, lonely ride into the future.

"In the fall of 1906, my husband and I'd go down to the courthouse and go into the judge's chambers and listen to political speeches."

Birdie Farmer could see this scene clearly in her mind.

"C. N. Haskell was running for the Democratic nomination for governor. Any time he was there, his name was mentioned, we'd have quite a crowd. The white folks were in the court-room, but I was in the chamber.

"In one of his campaign speeches, Haskell made the assertion that they were not to mention anything about the Negro or Jim Crow or anything until after the constitution was signed by the president, who was then Theodore Roosevelt. Because if they did, Theodore Roosevelt would certainly not sign it, and they couldn't become a state. They would wait until after the first assembly of the legislature to pass any kind of laws against the Negro, then they could do as they pleased.

"And, oh, that pleased them!"

Birdie Farmer clapped her hands.

"They gave vent to their feelings by throwing up their hats and just hollering and whooping.

"They didn't mention anything about restrictive laws at all. It was only after the first house and senate met, they did the dirty work, so to speak.

"The first senate bill was separate coaches. 'There shall be separate coaches for Negroes and whites.' And the separate coach the Negroes were put in was just a little place right in front of the train. Right next to the baggage car. It was not very comfortable. Wasn't kept clean."

The old woman's face grew tired. Her shoulders sagged.

"It made you feel that you weren't human, that's all."

Clara Luper picked up the thread of her conversation. Mrs. Luper, a history teacher, had led the first sit-ins in Oklahoma.

"In order to bring about changes, real changes, I think we had to go back to the Scripture, which teaches us plainly that, 'a little child shall lead them.' Our children helped us win our right to eat in restaurants, sleep in hotels. But more importantly, we used our children to remind people what America was all about."

She, too, stopped. Her dreams lay scattered about her like the daisies.

"The thing that hurts me most was not the fact that I went to jail twenty-three times trying to eat in an all-white restaurant, not the fact that once a man spit in my face. It was the day that our local amusement park opened to blacks. I was so happy because as a mother I wanted to take them to the park.

"So, when I found it was opened, I immediately contacted my daughter and said, 'Marilyn, I would like to take you to the park.' But Marilyn looked at me and said, 'Mom, I want to go to the park, but I would rather go with my friends.'

"And I realized that although I had spent my life trying to open up that park, I would never have the pleasure of taking my own children."

The group sat in silence until a night wind flipped a page in Charlie Ellison's hymnal.

"Well, that's it," he said. "Yeah, that's it. My eyes are about gone. Yeah, they're old. Too old. I can't see no more to tell."

TWO

Opportunity in the Land

"... *you just got to have the guts to get up and look for it.*"

JIM CAREY

The Honeymoon Trail

ST. GEORGE, UTAH
(1982)

The memories of men are too fragile a fabric to hang history from. The West that was is different from what we see in the movies. The Old West was America's forge, and the pioneers who passed through it had spirits of hammered steel. They were common people, made uncommon by hardship and by the endless thumping of noise and wind and dust. They felt a kinship with the dust. It surrounded them as, alone, their ragged, rusty wagon trains threaded across the plains.

Of all the Western trails, none was more unusual or more special than this. When the Mormons first settled in Arizona, the nearest temple was four hundred miles away in St. George, Utah. Each fall—after the harvest—young couples would get up a wagon train and head off to get married. The challenge of the trail, the hard knocks, seemed to seal the marriages stronger than ever. There were few divorces. One hundred and five years after its opening, people still come. It is the ultimate romantic journey. They call it the Honeymoon Trail.

Today a portion of that migration is reenacted each September. Descendants of those first honeymooners and a smattering of tourists trek the final seventy-five miles in farm wagons fitted with hoops and canvas. The caravan creaks out of Pipe Springs National Monument and winds across the old Arizona strip, north of the Grand Canyon, past Lost Mountain and Moccasin Peaks, down the rugged switchbacks of the Rock Canyon Dugway and under the Hurricane Cliffs into St. George. There is not another soul for hundreds of miles. Each year, the wagon train is led by a young Mormon couple who will be married in the St. George Temple at the end of the trip, a couple who are willing to test their love.

"Do you think there's many snakes out here?" asked the girl dressed in gingham. She was scuffing through the sagebrush, kicking dust with her Adidas.

Wagons on the Honeymoon Trail

"Nah," said the boy, who was holding tightly to her waist. "Snakes like to spend the night in ruts along the road."

She thumped his cowboy hat. "What road!" she squealed.

They were surrounded by an endless desert touched with the sun's red silver. Two tiny lines of dirt—a half-forgotten trail— had brought them to this place.

The boy took a shovel and began to turn the soil.

"You'll be okay," he said, breaking the clods to soften their bed.

Six dozen people spread across the prairie were doing the same thing. Their caravan had circled for the evening.

The girl, Lisa Hafen, looked toward the campfire and said, "I feel sorry for those pioneer women having to wear long dresses. If they only knew of Levi's back then, they would have changed for sure. I know they would have!"

The sun was nearly gone. The hills were all watercolor. The boy, Paul Reber, flicked a lizard off Lisa's dress. She screamed, then cuddled close and shared a laugh.

Lisa Hafen is the only daughter of a high school football coach in Kanab, Utah. She had vowed she wouldn't marry until she was twenty-three, but when Paul Reber proposed on horseback, she agreed—three years early. He is studying petroleum management. She is a child counselor. They met in college.

Lisa and Paul are Mormons. Riding the Honeymoon Trail was his idea. They soon learned that this was not just a trip into the past; it was a trip into themselves.

"You read about pioneers coming across the plains in covered wagons and handcarts," said Paul, "but you don't really have a feel for what they did until you ride one of those things for four or five straight hours." He rubbed his face. "Gets you worn down, tired, windburned, sunburned, hungry . . ."

"Ugh!" cried Lisa. "I've got sand between my teeth."

"Never smile into the dust," laughed Paul.

The past is caught up in the thousand winds that blow out here. Memories shorten the long hours.

"I could feel the blood running down my icy chest," said the man by the fire.

It was nighttime now, and smoke curled past unblinking eyes. "I knew if I reached any farther . . ."

The children around him leaned closer.

". . . he was going to *kill* me!"

Far off, a horse stamped in the darkness.

". . . and then . . . I awoke . . . and found I had been dreaming."

Sighs and laughter floated out over the prairie. Coyotes picked up the sound and sang it to each other.

Suddenly came more music—not a harmonica or a guitar—a symphonic swell from under the canvas of a covered wagon.

A voice, deep and rich, said, ". . . Cinderella wanted desperately to go to the ball. . . ."

A six-year-old, Laycee Mangum, was sprawled next to a Coleman lantern, listening to a battery-powered storyteller. She was half asleep, clutching a tape-recorded dream.

Such were the tickets that took folks through the night.

At sunrise, it was cold on the prairie. A couple of kids left the comfort of the campfire, looking for a bathroom. There was none. They tripped across the plains toward the high grass.

The meadow was a huge and birdless silence. Outside the ancient wagons stood two pieces of pink American Tourister luggage that matched the morning sky.

Rookie teamsters began to clatter about, working on the tangled harnesses. The "trail boss," Mel Heaton, fixed a broken wagon wheel with bailing wire. The "pioneers" had forgotten to bring axle grease, so the wheel had been soaking in a mud hole all night.

One exasperated driver got hopelessly lost in his snarled rigging. "Let's get a knife and cut it!" he cried. Another laughed as his group began harnessing and said, "Yesterday this part was on the front of the horse!"

Lisa was at the back of her wagon, repairing the first day's damage. Not the wagon's—hers. She had broken a nail. Paul brought her a bouquet of wildflowers. She climbed inside the carriage to rummage for a comb. Her horse ate the bouquet.

The trip had not started well.

"I lost her wedding ring on the trail yesterday," Paul confided. "But I found it."

He pointed back over the path they had come.

"We rode three hours, and I can still see where we left."

Lisa came out, struggling into a pair of sweatpants. Bloomers had looked prettier beneath her long pioneer dress, but sweat pants were warmer.

"It's not as windy today," comforted Paul.

Lisa laughed. "The West would have been settled twenty years earlier if the pioneers didn't have to go back for their hats."

The two shared a few quiet moments together in the lee of the prairie schooner and then broke camp. The modern world vanished. Big Belgian horses strained in their traces, and the wagons clattered away. Children waved their hats. Outriders raced back and forth. The caravan rolled west across Pipe Valley under a cloudless sky. Lisa tried to keep a journal, but the ride was too bumpy. Comfort was not a word she would have written down. Her only convenience, four layers of foam rubber on the wagon seat, didn't help.

The journey to the temple lasted four more days. Seventy miles. Near the end, the trail turned so crooked it could have run for the legislature, finally disappearing completely over the side of a canyon. The women got out and walked. The men lowered the wagons by rope.

"You have to really *want* to get married," said Paul in a masterful understatement. That morning, he went fifteen hundred feet—mostly straight down.

The next day, the caravan was back under the golden arches of McDonald's, passing through the modern tunnels of the interstate.

Paul and Lisa were in the lead wagon—she holding a handful of prairie flowers, he searching for the temple's spire. In back,

Paul Reber and Lisa Hafen on the Trail

Laycee Mangum wore an old dress her great-grandmother had made and listened again to her storyteller's tape: "Oh, Beauty, we'll be together forever . . ."

Dogs ran out to bark, then inspected with puzzled faces wheels not made of rubber.

Twelve hundred wedding guests lined the streets.

"There's my uncle!" yelled Lisa.

"Hey, Paul," said a man on the sidewalk. "Smile!"

Click!

Trail-weary faces were shown around like merit badges. The procession finally pulled to a stop at the temple, looking for all the world like Cinderella's coach—at one minute past midnight.

". . . and she and the prince lived happily ever after," said the voice from the tape recorder.

"Oh, brother," moaned the little girl. "That's corny."

Over the Next Hill

One of the first Americans to walk these Western hills said, "We love the quiet. We listen to the birds play. When the prairie is rustled by the wind, we wonder if the ground has anything to say."

In time, it would.

Four-and-a-half-billion barrels of oil bubble under the east Texas grass—an oil field twice the size of Connecticut. In the fall of 1981, pipe trucks and drilling rigs rumbled over these rises to create a rush hour in small-town streets. Traffic cops wrote six hundred tickets a month. People were chasing an oil boom such as the West had not seen in years. Giddings, Texas, fifty miles east of Austin, was the center of all that activity—a two-headed magnet pulling those in need of a future, pushing those who clung to the past. Twenty-five hundred people came looking for jobs, nearly doubling the town's population in less than a year. Housing was hard to find. Imagination was not. One man turned oil tanks on their sides and made a motel. Some people slept in cars or in abandoned buildings. Most, like Jim and Debra Cary and their daughter, Chastity, merely pitched a tent and camped out. The Carys had been farmers until they went broke.

"When I went into hogs," said Jim, "they were sixty-six dollars a hundred. The first group I sold went for twenty-five. I had to beg a guy to get that."

Jim left the farm and a low-paying job back East to look for work in the oil fields.

"Money's on the rigs," said Jim. "You won't find it anyplace else, not without experience."

The Carys went derrick to derrick, nine hundred miles, looking for work.

"A lot of people wouldn't do that," said Jim. "I know a lot of people wouldn't do it. Like my parents, they think I'm a little bit off for not staying on the farm. But Debra doesn't mind. And I don't mind. And our little daughter, she loves it. As long as she's with us, and she's happy, that's what matters."

Being broke in a boomtown isn't the best. But it's better than what the Carys had before.

"I know a guy here," said Jim, looking around at the other families whose tents dotted the campsite. "He got down to eighty-five cents in his pocket before he got a job."

The Carys see success where others see failure, sunshine where others see shadow and storm.

"I think it's like old times," said Debra as a brief shower sent the family scurrying to their tent. "People done it years ago, heading West trying to find something better."

Deposits at the Giddings bank jumped from $16 million to $85 million. City employees got a 41 percent raise to keep them from giving up their jobs and going to the oil fields.

All this did not bring honey-colored happiness. The cost of living rose faster than a gusher. Jim made $8.20 an hour when he worked. He did not work much.

"There's still opportunity in this land," said Jim, tossing his hard hat and lunch box into the car, "but you just got to have guts enough to get up and look for it. There's jobs. Lots of people up North say there ain't jobs. Just pack your gear, you'll find one. You go far enough, you'll find one."

He drove out the main gate of the campground where the Carys had pitched their tent. A park ranger waved.

"There's a more immediate problem," said Jim. "Texas state parks allow families to stay only two weeks." Campgrounds are not meant to be neighborhoods.

"What are you going to do after fourteen days?" I asked.

"Go to another park," said Jim. "If it takes a couple of years, we're going to be here a couple of years."

"Moving from campground to campground?"

"Moving from campground to campground."

The farm family that loved its roots now has none. On Chastity's birthday, they checked general delivery at the post office.

"Nope, sorry, nothing," said the man behind the counter.

They spent the day on a wind-rumpled hill. There was not much of a party, only two gifts—a watermelon and a dog named Freeman. The family looked within to find its home.

"You think you've found your dream yet?" I asked.

"No," said Jim. "We're still looking."

"We'll know when we find it," said Debra.

Within a year, the oil boom trickled away. The recession cut deeper. Jim won and lost six jobs—six jobs in three different states.

"I could have scratched a snake's belly on a stepladder. You keep trying. You keep trying. Pretty soon, you just want to throw up your hands and say, 'Forget it. I'll just mooch off of everybody else.' But it doesn't work that way," Jim said.

"We lived with my uncle back in Indiana for a while. Debbie wanted another child. I did too. You can't have that in a tent."

The family then moved to Colorado.

"We stayed with my aunt for three weeks," said Debbie. "But there was no work, so back we went to Indiana."

Jim found several part-time jobs. It was less expensive to live there. A barber in nearby Wallace, Indiana, charged a buck a haircut—$1.50 if you couldn't get there before sundown.

"Someday, Deb, I'll buy us a home," said Jim. "Build it just the way you like it." The couple pushed a baby stroller through a ring of leaves. Their daughter, Chastity, ran ahead. They were looking at houses.

"Only trouble," he touched her shoulder, "I'd have to have ten jobs to pay for it."

"I wouldn't see you much," said Debra, slipping her arm through his. The wind stirred. She drew close to him. Chastity spotted a park.

"Come on!" she cried.

The family rolled the stroller across the street and disappeared. So, it seemed, did their dream.

But that fall two things happened. Jim got a call from the Soil Conservation Service. A job! And the bank approved his home loan.

In the evening, there was a party. It was Debra's twenty-eighth birthday.

A big harvest moon felt its way through the clouds. The family held hands around a table. Jim gave a quiet benediction.

"Like my grandfather told me, you can't make it all in one night and be set up for the rest of your life. It's going to be slow, but Lord willing, we'll make it."

They dropped hands. Jim glanced out at the moon.

"If things start looking down, Debbie and I still have our tent. We still got our camper. We'll take off."

Sweat Equity

Folks out here in farm country say they learn to work from "can to can't"—from sunup to sunset—a way of life as natural to them as the rolling hills. Each man planting, each man reaping the benefit of his constant labor. That old-time farm philosophy seems somehow out of step with our march toward the thirty-five-hour work week. It would *never* work with today's big business—or would it?

David Stauffacher grew up on a small Wisconsin dairy farm. He is now chairman of the board of a $12 million motel chain. His construction crew and most of his stockholders call him "Dad." His daughter, Beth, drives the heavy equipment. David, Jr., oversees the building crew. Brother Scotty *is* the crew. There are ten, ten kids in all. Each summer, they race the wind, building motels for half of what it costs their competition.

"I wanted to teach them to struggle," said their father. "I

think that's good for them. Then they'll understand when they spend the buck what went into making that dollar."

The children get no allowance and little salary. But they do get a percentage of each motel once it is in operation—a sort of sweat equity.

"How much do you suppose you're worth?" I asked one of the boys.

He rested a hammer on his hip, looked up, and figured silently.

"After this one, a quarter of a million."

"And how old are you?"

"I'm twenty-four."

The sides of each motel are enclosed in six weeks. Six weeks later, the motel is open. The family works so fast that they can make a profit with only 50 percent occupancy. It helps that they also make almost all the furniture for the motels themselves. In winter, when it is too cold to work outside, David's wife, Pat, sews the bedspreads.

"We don't come to this job half-organized," said the senior Stauffacher. "Our house is full of organization. Our buildings are thought out. We've done the process a number of times. You won't see many guys around here with blueprints in their hands."

The secret is not speed alone. It is simplicity. Stauffacher uses a technique any child can master. Cement blocks are stacked against a temporary frame. The frame is then leveled so that each block does not have to be set individually. Inside walls go up in seven minutes instead of two hours. A stucco-like mixture of portland cement, lime, and fiberglass keeps it all together. The process has met every major building code. But, as you might expect, those who enforce the child-labor laws haunt the Stauffacher's construction sites. What do the kids think of a father who sneers at coffee breaks and allows only a half-hour for meals?

"When I was sixteen or seventeen," said Mark Stauffacher, "I thought my dad was the meanest guy, the strictest guy on the face of the earth. Looking back now, I really appreciate the things he's done. It kinda brings tears when I think about it."

The Stauffacher girls on the job

In summer, the family lives together in rented rooms near each site—the children, their wives, and their children.

"I don't have to take time out at night at the supper table and sit down and worry whether I'm spending ten minutes with my children," said David Stauffacher. "The family farmer never worried about that. He worried if the sun was up and if the hay was in the barn and the cows milked and are we going to make it next year."

No one could maintain this pace forever. There is just a summer season. But there is a season—and the Stauffachers are a team.

"I like to feel that we could take anybody on," said the senior Stauffacher, "apples for apples in this business, right here today, and beat them. If these boys want to pick this thing up and go with it some day when I get too tired or too old, fine. If they say to me, 'Hey, I've had enough,' that's okay, too, because I'm convinced the majority of these kids know their capabilities now. They know what they can do. They could never come back and look me in the eye and say, 'Hey, we can't compete in the outside world,' because they can."

David Stauffacher, an American farmer, is a man who planted his dream—in his family.

A Man's Home...

Mort Copenhaver works long hours at a dental clinic in Phoenix. But when he has time, he dreams. Not so unusual, really. We all have dreams, but Mort Copenhaver built his. Each evening, Dr. Copenhaver drives nine hundred feet up the side of Camelback Mountain to his own castle. It has six-foot-thick walls, battle towers, and a drawbridge. Inside, there are sixteen-foot ceilings, secret passageways, and, yes, a dungeon. But the furnishings are not from the late show. In the family room, there's a heated whirlpool that seats twenty; there's also a fifteen-foot waterfall, a billiards room, and a bedroom big enough for King Kong.

All this for two people—Mort and his girl friend, Beverly Rodrigues.

The dream did not come easily. When Copenhaver bought the land back in 1966, it wasn't level enough for a buzzard to land on, much less to build a castle on. Contractors said it would cost

$100,000 just to put in the driveway. So Mort built the road himself with a jackhammer and a truck. It took three years. The neighbor who lived below at the time wasn't too happy. He took Mort to court.

"Once I got the road past his house," said Dr. Copenhaver, "I had decided that I was going to build a castle that would dwarf his place."

He did. But it took thirteen years to chisel his home out of the mountain. Most of the time, Copenhaver worked alone. He had no formal training as an architect, but he read books. He figured that building a castle on the side of a mountain wasn't much different from planting a false tooth. So, for $4,000 down and $16,000 a year, Mort Copenhaver got twenty-five rooms on ten levels. He can afford to live in his castle because outdoor

Mort Copenhaver's castle

52

fountains recycle water used in his solar cooling system. The castle's electric bill runs about $100 a month.

Mort is not as rich as most castle owners, but he has something the rest of us do not—his house is paid for.

"I had to be very careful where I placed my electrical outlets," said Copenhaver. "I cut them into the granite, into the side of the mountain. Mountains don't let you change your mind."

Almost everything in the castle is a bargain.

"I buy things before they're needed," said Copenhaver. "The other day, I got a good deal on picture frames."

Four large wooden frames were hanging empty on the wall.

"You know anyone who can draw?"

Mort settled back onto his golden throne. Pushed himself up into its red crushed-velvet seat.

"This is just a prop," he said. His dangling legs did not touch the floor. "I'm just a regular guy."

Go-Cooker

ODESSA, TEXAS
(1979)

Rush hour in Odessa, Texas, has become kind of a moving McDonald's. There is more that sizzles here than just hot pavement. Hooked to the back bumper of several small cars in Odessa are little ovens that fry eggs on the way to work and steaks on the way home. The oven's heat comes from the car's exhaust pipe, which is shielded to keep out the fumes. Bill Worrell is the man responsible for this culinary revolution.

"I burned my leg pretty badly on an exhaust pipe one day," said Worrell, "so I got to thinking. If that thing can cook me, it can cook a potato. That's when I went to work."

Worrell's "Go-Cooker" costs about the same as ten tanks of gas. It bakes practically anything.

"How far would you have to go to cook a ham?" I asked as we rocketed down the interstate.

"How big a ham?" asked Worrell.

"Four or five pounder."

"Oh," he said, "I would imagine about seventy-five or eighty miles probably."

We swerved off an exit ramp and plowed down a dirt road. Great fantails of dust spouted behind. Dust doesn't seem to bother the Go-Cooker, but hills do.

"It takes a little longer if you're going downhill," said Worrell as we crested a ridge and shot down the other side, "about forty miles more."

Just the opposite, of course, if you're going uphill.

"I cooked a ham in about twenty miles, climbing a mountain in northern Colorado. We were really burning."

Friends say Worrell does tend to drive a bit faster when he's cooking.

"You can't do much baking when you're idling."

But no matter how fast he goes, there is still one problem: "Do you mind if we spin around the parking lot?" said Worrell, checking his rearview mirror. "It isn't soup yet."

Bill Worrell (in dark T-shirt) and hungry passers-by

Beehive Telephone

WESTERN UTAH
(1981)

I've often thought that the people who really know how to run this country are too busy pumping gas or cutting hair—regular folks with good ideas. Remember a few years back when people were trying to figure a way out of the gas shortage? My barber had a simple solution.

"You wanna save gas?" he said. "Do away with credit cards. Make 'em pay cash."

That man could send a committee to lunch.

America is full of such folks. Take Arthur Brothers. For most of his adult life, he has been planting telephones in places where Ma Bell never treads. He is a dreamer who believes in the right of every American to life, liberty, and the pursuit of a busy signal.

To find Art Brothers, you go west to Salt Lake City, turn left, and drive for the rest of your life. Along about middle age, you

56

may pass a battered 1951 Ford installer moving among the tumbleweeds. That is the Beehive Telephone Company.

"Well, you said you'd be here for breakfast," said the woman on a remote wind-swept plain. "You missed breakfast. I guessed you'd be here by dinner."

"Ah, two hundred fifty miles isn't far," said Brothers, jumping from his truck.

Art Brothers has only a handful of customers scattered over an area the size of Massachusetts. Big phone companies have simply passed them by.

"They forgot that we were still in the United States," said one man, leaning against a fence. "There's only a few of us out here, lots of dogs and cats, and I think about fifty-nine people."

Brothers took up the challenge because he works cheaply. He is to Ma Bell what a junk man is to Bloomingdale's. Almost everything he has is recycled. He even types his letters onto the backs of letters people send him.

His is no cushy life of emptying phone boxes. The Beehive switchboard—old enough to remember Audie Murphy—is in his mobile home. In sixteen years, he has not made a profit. For most of that time, he has worked alone, living on $400 a month.

"Sure, I could earn a lot of money," said Brothers, "if I went to work for a big corporation. But I don't know if they could stand me."

Brothers is something of a bureaucratic renegade. The Federal Aviation Administration suspended his pilot's license when he landed on a highway to repair telephone poles. The Federal Communications Commission called him on the carpet for letting the madam of a Nevada bordello use his emergency radio.

"None of the calls from this brothel were used for prostitution," said Brothers. "They all related to the safety of life and property. But the chairman of the FCC raised up and said, 'Mr. Brothers, is a call to a liquor distributor an emergency?' And I says, 'Mr. Chairman, if you owned a w———— that's run out of booze, *that's* an emergency.' "

57

Brothers got back into the good graces of the law by fixing a special telephone hookup under some sagebrush for Deputy Sheriff Phil Hecketthorn. Now the sheriff doesn't have to drive ninety miles to talk to his office.

Brothers would like to string a line to the nearby town of Eskdale, Utah. It has the only ambulance in the desert valley, but for years the poles have stopped eight miles short of town while the government considers his petition to cross federal land.

"Washington says I would be disturbing the 'beauty' of the Great Utah Salt Flats. Good gosh! Folks've only driven across seventy miles of desert when they reach here. I would think they would like to see approaching civilization."

Brothers threw up his hands.

"Then they could say, 'I've made it.'"

Art Brothers was born, perhaps, a century too late. He would have felt more at home laying track for the first transcontinental railroad.

"Hello, Mabel? Art. Yeah, just about done. Couple more spikes . . ."

The sun slipped behind the mountains. Brothers and his truck and his telephone pole cast the only shadows.

"Yeah. See ya. Be home in about six hours."

"I'm an orphan," said Brothers, rolling up the wire on his patch phone. "I never had anything all my life. I've always done with what I could find."

That kind of corporate style should someday reward Art Brothers with a profit. Maybe—he'd even print a yellow page.

"*Jump So High...*"

In the Brooklyn of the early 1950s, a boy who wanted to be in ballet was about as popular as the chicken pox. Eliot Feld hid his dance slippers in a brief case so his neighbors would think he had an ordinary job. In time, he became one of America's finest ballet choreographers, but looking back, it would have been easier if he'd had a friend around who looked like Mr. T.

Ballet is still out of the question for most of the children in his old neighborhood. It costs too much: $100 for shoes; $60 a week for lessons; about $76,000 to prepare for a career.

Six years ago, Eliot Feld began to consider the talent that goes untapped. Ballet recruiters never came to his school. Scholarships for children with ability often came too late for them to make it as professionals. Ballet careers usually begin at the age of seven or eight.

Feld persuaded the New York City public school system to

let him audition thousands of children—both boys and girls—so he could select the most promising, and set up classes to develop professional dancers. He did not recruit from the specialized schools for performing arts. He traveled to the public classrooms to look for ordinary eight-year-olds.

Today he is back in his old neighborhood, searching for talent.

"The school yard looks tiny to me."

It is covered with snow. People scurry along the sidewalks. Heads down. Children scamper off school buses and race up concrete stairs into the warm building. A crowd of kids has begun to form outside the auditorium. Eliot Feld and his assistants have set up a table inside to begin judging. Feld is a slight man, dressed much like the students who will come before him. There are flecks of gray in his hair, but he has an eight-year-old's smile.

"Okay, let them in," he says.

Children straggle down the aisle and wind up the stairs to the stage. A pianist begins a steady stream of music.

Feld shouts, "Slide the foot!"

Long lines of children begin to jiggle. The place begins to take on the smell of a locker room after recess.

Clapping his hands, Feld hops up onto the stage.

"Now, run to me and *jump! Good* boy! Good boy!"

The children laugh and skip into his arms. One little fellow with a shock of hair that points off to Connecticut misses every beat, but Feld is captivated.

"Some of the kids are not slick and athletic, but they have a sparkle in their eyes," he says later. "Something special."

The youngster is called back for a second look. He will get to see how dreams are made.

"Up! Up! First position! Point your feet!"

Dreams are not made easily.

"Pick up those knees! Bend those knees! Up! Up!"

Advanced students train four days a week, twice on Saturdays. It takes almost all their free time.

"If they don't have a passion for it," says Feld, "they go

away. And they should. They should. Because you can't dance unless it is at the center of your life."

Feld and his assistants have auditioned more than one hundred thousand children from every public school in New York City. They teach only one in eighty-three. This is not another social welfare program. Those who are accepted get subway tokens uptown, costumes, and instruction.

"What's in it for you?" I wonder, as Feld hops down from the stage. He looks at the departing children.

"Dancers," he says simply.

Later, two small boys skip through the chilling cold on a sidewalk dusted with snow.

"I can't wait to get home," says one. "It's freezing."

Large gray buildings block out the sky above them. Hissing steam vents seem to bring the clouds to street level. The older boy stops. Spins. The younger one repeats the step, adding an extra twist as he slides on a patch of ice. They both laugh and hurry into the subway.

Marcus Felix and his pal, Rafael Cordero, won tickets uptown from the stark pavement of the Bedford Stuyvesant public housing projects. Marcus is one of the bright ones—one of the promising ones. He came with the first group of children when he was just seven years old. Ballet has opened a world beyond Bedford Stuyvesant. He has traveled to eleven cities as a professional dancer, has seen Niagara Falls, and has visited the White House.

Marcus Felix is ten years old. He lives with his grandmother in a neighborhood where all they have is hope. The world no longer seems lost and lonely to him. He paints his own landscape with muscle and imagination.

The little body arches above the wooden floor. Legs spin, land, and spring again—arms stretch, as if to catch the shadow reflected in the practice mirror. At last, the music stops, and Marcus drops down next to the piano.

"When I jump real high," he sighs, "I feel like I'm going to hit the ceiling." A deep breath. "That's what I want to do." A smile. "One day jump so high, I'll hit my head on the ceiling."

It is all the world he wants.

It'll happen.

Texas Tycoons

HUNT, TEXAS
(1982)

Remember the first *real* money you ever made? Not the weekly welfare dole from your parents—I mean cash from a stranger. I remember my first coin. I was trying to sell lemonade. Two cents a glass; a penny if you brought back the cup so I could re-use the ice. My first customer was an old man from down the block. He gave me a dime, which I quickly traded to my brother for a nickel because it was bigger. Brother Bill became a salesman. I became a reporter. Bill would have fit right in here in Hunt, Texas.

We have stopped by for a stockholder's meeting at Hunt Elementary School. Michael Hailey is president of the company. The corporate limo is a school bus. Quite logical really . . . the entire company consists of fifth- and sixth-grade school children. They are the youngest members of the chamber of commerce.

Their corporation is no mere classroom exercise. The kids run a $20,000-a-year business. It has made possible all sorts of

63

extras for their school—a new drama department, a copying machine, a lighting system, electronic school bells, and gym shorts for all seventy-eight children.

"Hi, Tom."

That's president Hailey, age eleven, talking on his private telephone. The kids also have their own letterhead.

"How are things in Washington?"

He's speaking to Congressman Tom Loeffler.

Mike Hailey represents the local chamber of commerce.

"See these business cards," he says, shuffling a stack in his hand. "People will pay attention when you give them one of these cards. They won't just walk off and pick their teeth with them. Let me write you up for five hundred."

The students seem to have no problem making money. Hunt isn't a big place, but some of the kids built their own candy stand. Others manufacture the Texas Hill Country Weather Rock. The instructions, which the children wrote, say that when the weather rock is wet, "it's raining." When the rock is dry, "it is not." When it starts to cough, "there is too much air pollution."

Don't laugh. The rocks have made them a $4,000 profit.

When Mike Hailey goes looking for a loan, he sees the bank president.

"How much could we borrow for our corporation?"

"Well," says the bank president, looking over his records, "two or three thousand dollars, I suspect."

"The name of the game is money," says Tracy Gilbreth, the teacher who started the kids' company nine years ago. "I watch 'em, but I let them run it."

Class business is in addition to regular studies. Anyone who handles cash must have an "A" in math. Kids who don't do their homework go on unemployment.

Why did the children pick Mike to be president?

"Hailey has a reputation for getting things done," says Gilbreth. "In less than eight months, the class has cleared $15,000."

Does the pressure of all that responsibility get too great some time?

"The only time I really relax my brain," says Mike, "is at night."

Well, not all the kids dream of balanced books.

"What do you want to be when you get into fifth grade?" I ask a small boy who is lounging against a computer.

He looks past the girl who is furiously tabulating the day's receipts, then returns to his screen. Alien ships are closing in on his quarter.

"A bounty hunter."

But business does have its perks. Mike gets an occasional two-ice-cream-cone lunch and a lot of solid training.

"See," says Mike when we meet over a dish of fudge ripple, "what we try to do is go into every place and always come out with something."

"By the way," I ask, "who's paying for this?"

"Ya'll," he says.

"That's a Little Cheaper..."

Manny Gammage has a motto: "Quality is like buying oats. If you want good clean oats, you've got to pay a fair price. If you want oats that's already run through the horse, that's a little cheaper."

Each day, Manny's shop in Austin, Texas, fills with folks who are mighty picky about their oats, people who are looking for something unique. Manny Gammage is one of the last of this country's custom hatmakers.

He creates personalities. Requests come from all over the world. If you can describe it, Manny can make it.

"Let me read you the first paragraph of this letter I got from Burma," says Manny. 'Okay, I'm a big, ugly, tattooed son of a gun with twenty-six years in the army and I'm queer for hats. I wanna hat made that will scare women and children and start fights in Wyoming bars.' " Gammage roars with laughter.

"We fixed him up with somethin' similar to a derby. I put

a silver and turquoise hatband on it. I figured that would start a fight in any bar just about anywhere."

Manny's hats begin at ninety dollars. They come with more options than a new car—rattlesnake hatbands, feathers, a gold toothpick with a diamond—but he is not just another rich man's tailor. Manny could charge a lot more. He likes the mix of cowboys and college kids who come into his store. Each gets the same patient treatment and the chance to get something exactly as he wants it.

But . . . no one gets it quickly. Manny makes only twenty-five hats a day. Everything is hand-steamed, hand-stamped, and hand-sewn. His tools are so old, that he has to go to a museum for parts.

Why doesn't he just put in a couple of modern machines?

"I might could," says Manny, "but I'm not going to. I have no ambition at all to go into some kind of mass production. If I

Manny Gammage surrounded by his hats

can't finish it myself and look at it and approve of it, then I don't want to do it."

Gammage measures success not in money but in the lives he has reached. His walls are lined with pictures of people who have his hats. Each sparks a memory.

"The first time I saw him," says Gammage, looking at a photograph of a man sporting a huge ten-gallon hat, "he had on a suit and tie. We fixed him up with a rig that started him down the road to destruction."

He is talking about Marion Rice Zetzman, one of the busiest doctors in Texas. Zetzman is an author, an educator, and "He can throw a tommy-hawk better than anyone in Dallas," giggled Gammage.

Well, that's not exactly true. Some folks would say that the best tomahawk thrower is a guy named Billy Bob Oafley. That's because Billy Bob and Marion Rice Zetzman are the same person. After Dr. Zetzman bought one of Manny's hats, he found fun beyond the golf course.

"Turkey feathers and deer tracks make mighty thin soup," said the good doctor as he lurched after his tomahawk.

"I started changing my name to Billy Bob on weekends so I could mix with folks I would never meet as a doctor."

People like Brazos Bailey, for instance.

"I'm a quarter-blood Choctaw Indian and full-blood hacksaw," said Bailey, gnawing on a soup bone. "I can cut anything."

Or like Wrong Lodge Watkins.

"Some fellows in Colorado introduced me to what they call a 'Bent's Fort Special,'" says Watkins. "That's apple cider mixed with 130-proof Ever Clear. I didn't know what I was drinking. We drank three gallons between the six of us one night, and I wound up sleeping in the wrong man's lodge. That's how I got the name Wrong Lodge."

Marion Zetzman is one doctor whose idea of a Saturday afternoon foursome is just a bit different. His weekend camp near Jewitt, Texas, is a long way from the country club. But thanks to Manny's hat, Billy Bob fits right in. For years, few people

Billy Bob Oafley

Hidy to Bob "Boots" Dotson NBC News from a man and his dog!

Billy Bob O. at the Rocking L Ranch

knew of Zetzman's dual existence. He agreed to reveal his double life only after he was reminded that John Wayne was also called Marion. Actually, no one seemed to mind when they found out that Billy Bob was chief of community medicine at the University of Texas. It prompted Brazos Bailey to confess that he owns a store in Dallas. Wrong Lodge announced that he repairs vending machines. They, too, camp only on weekends.

"Billy Bob is a simple, barefooted country boy from Roscoe, Texas, with a Ph.D.," says Zetzman. "Things are too tense. Too uptight. And when they get that way, you've gotta have some outlet to relax."

Wrong Lodge tips dangerously near the campfire with a half-empty jug of Ever Clear in his hand. The doctor turns to look, then tugs his ten-gallon hat down over his ears.

"There are more people out there who have Billy Bobs," he says, "than you'll ever know about."

THREE

Give Us Your Tired, Your Poor

"...telling him of dreams they will not live."
BOB DOTSON

The Sunshine Child

Perhaps this story would be better told at bedtime. It deals with wishes and dreams and things kids hold dear. Any child can tell you the plot. It begins with, "Once upon a time," and it is true.

"Take my hand, now. Oh, you're a good little girl." The heavy-set policeman sits in a circle of kids. He is patrolman Bill Sample. For nine years, Sample has been stationed at a Philadelphia children's hospital. His beat takes him among children who are very sick. He smiles and they listen, telling him of dreams they will not live.

Bill Sample decided to buy some of those dreams. He and his wife, Helene, and some of their friends sent one child on a trip to touch the snow. Another to see the redwood trees. The Samples' lives soon filled with letters of dreams that had come true.

"Jody had never seen the ocean," says Helene, reading from a thank-you note they had received from a child's parent. "What a joy to see her eyes light up with awe and wonder." Helene's eyes well over.

"These letters always make me cry."

Sample wraps his arm around his wife's shoulder.

"That little girl will keep a thousand memories in her head," he says. "She does more for our lives than we could possibly do for hers."

Sample is nearly always surrounded by kids. Doctors refer their "special" children to him.

"I guess that's the only fairy tale in the book," says Sample, holding in his lap a tiny girl with deep brown eyes and button nose. Her name is Christina Wilson. She has leukemia. Her dream is to meet a mouse named Minnie.

"I wanna kiss her," says Christina, leaning her face toward the page.

"You will," says Sample.

He set about raising the money necessary to send Christina to a land beyond her storybooks—to a land where Minnie Mouse actually lives. She and her entire family went to Disneyland.

"I haven't ridden on Dumbo for hours and hours and hours," said Christina, pointing to an amusement ride with large gray elephants circling high overhead, "Let's go again." Her small hand was the only concession she gave her parents, who struggled to keep up.

"There's Donald!" she squealed. "Hi, Donald. Hi, Mickey."

Christina joined the crush of kids trying to touch their heroes.

"Have you seen Minnie?" she asked.

Her question was lost in the babble of voices. The fifty children around the Disney characters all felt compelled to tell their life stories at once. A big round foot in high-heeled shoes stepped up behind Christina. She caught a glimpse of a thin black tail. She whirled.

"Minnie!"

74

There are some moments in life that develop slowly like Polaroid pictures. After all the anticipation and the longing, after all the nights filled with dreams, Christina gasped and touched Minnie's cheek. She didn't move. In Christina's hand was a small see-through purse with a picture of Minnie Mouse. The real Minnie, the one who stood before her, held out her arms. Christina did not hesitate. She jumped up and fell into the big white hands that stretched out to greet her.

They held each other for almost a full minute; then Christina leaned back to look at Minnie's face.

"Hi, Minnie," her voice was barely a whisper.

The mouse said nothing, but nudged Christina's cheek.

"Minnie, I love you."

Christina's parents glanced at each other. The crowd grew

A kiss for Minnie

quiet. The little girl bent slowly at the waist, as if trying to reach someone standing on the other side of a fence. Minnie kneeled down. Her shiny black nose came close, and in a twinkling, Christina kissed it.

Bill Sample was not there. He was back in Philadelphia, sitting alone at his dining-room table. Outside, the season's first snowfall fell silently. It was getting dark. He was still in uniform, just home from work. A stack of thank-you notes was piled next to some leftover casserole on the table. The food was growing cold. Sample was reading.

Bill Sample seldom takes a vacation himself, but in a sense, he travels with every child he touches. To the parents, many of whose life savings have been drained by their children's illnesses, Bill Sample is a miracle worker—a man who brings joy when hope is gone.

Bill Sample's Sunshine Foundation now has chapters in fourteen cities.

For nearly three thousand children, dreams have come true.

Antique Courage

HARLEM, NEW YORK
(1984)

Morning sun streams into a darkened room. A little boy turns on his pillow. A little girl looks for a teddy bear lost in the night. The sun slants to a stack of toys tossed in the corner and comes to rest on a doll whose face is smudged with play. The boy wakes. Rubs his eyes. Watches a sliver of dust soar past wallpaper balloons. An abandoned baby bottle lies among the covers. Others in the room begin to stir. One by one, little heads rise up from a dozen cribs. And cry.

Childhood should be a season of sun—of dreams—but these children awake each morning from an American nightmare. They were born addicted to drugs.

Raphael Frazier's mother had passed on her $400-a-day heroin and cocaine habit. Emerald Alexander ate paint and added lead poisoning to her tragedy.

"Good morning!"

Hundreds of such children have been saved by Clara Hale. She stands straight, like a teacher ignoring a bus-load of grief. This Mother's Day, she will be seventy-nine.

"Hello, angel."

Mrs. Hale scuffs from bed to bed, holding her tattered bathrobe tightly at the neck. She is bone thin, elderly, but unstooped, a woman who faces life with antique courage.

"Hello, precious. What's the matter with you?"

Clara bends to help Raphael, who is searching for the heel in his sock. It is hiding on top of his foot. He reaches for the discarded baby bottle in his crib and sticks it in his mouth. His crying stops.

"All of them don't have to die," says Mama Hale, stroking the boy's hair, "because some of them have the determination to live."

"Hold me, Mama Hale!"

The old woman in the tattered bathrobe crosses to Emerald Alexander, pulls her up, and pats her gently.

"Come on, children. Get dressed. We're going to the park."

Clara Hale lives in a neighborhood of burned-out homes, once beautiful brick buildings, now mostly boarded up. Some have gaping black holes where windows have been poked out many times and are now outlined in soot. They stare down at Mama Hale's little band of toddlers skipping along the sidewalk.

"Look out where you're walking so you won't fall down," says Mrs. Hale, lifting Raphael over an old mattress and kicking aside a rusting can. A large dog snarls. The children grab hands and pass on.

"Oh, look at that building," says Mama Hale surveying the street. "Isn't it a shame how they let that go?"

A woman sways drunkenly at the street corner. A black cat sitting on a window sill blinks silently in the sun. Two people huddle together in a nearby doorway. A crumpled wad of bills is passed. A small plastic bag of white powder is pressed into a jacket. Clara Hale's neighborhood is all selling and consuming, a cattleshoot for drugs.

The children of these streets learn early that life is unfair. Clara Hale shows them it can be lovely, too.

"We're going over here," says Mama Hale, shepherding her small flock through a chain link fence into the park. The children break and run for the slide. Mrs. Hale stands guard near the bottom.

She did not set out to do saintly things. In fact, she was retiring fifteen years ago when a drug-addicted mother left her baby at the door. Mrs. Hale took it in, and word got around. Soon her tiny apartment was jammed with cribs.

She had already spent a lifetime caring for other people's children. Her husband had died early, and she supported her family by raising forty neighborhood kids. She had three of her own. All forty-three went to college. They all graduated. She agreed to care for these new babies on one condition: that their mothers enter drug rehabilitation programs. She did not want to send these children back to mean streets. Four hundred ninety-seven drug-afflicted babies have now passed through her home. All but eleven were returned to their mothers.

Raphael's mother, Nancy Frazier, didn't think people like Mrs. Hale existed anymore.

"She used to talk to me all the time, and she would say, 'Nancy, you could be anything that you wanted to be.'"

Because of Mama Hale, Nancy Frazier is kicking her $400-a-day habit.

"Mama Hale! Catch me!" screams Raphael, giggling down the crowded slide. Nancy's eyes flick to her son, hold, then focus somewhere beyond.

"She helped me grow, too."

That afternoon as the children prepare for their nap, I ask Mama Hale, "Have you ever wondered if you'd run out of love?"

A baby in her arms coos softly as she leans back in the old rocker that rests near her bed.

"I think if I ran out of love, I'd be out of life," says Mama Hale as she kisses the little thumb.

She places the child in her crib and draws the shutters closed. The room darkens.

"Here is your teddy bear," says Mama Hale, tucking the cover around still another child.

"That ain't no teddy bear," says the small voice beneath the blanket. "That's an elephant."

"Oh, I'm sorry," says Mama Hale, tucking in the elephant. "Goodnight, sweetie. I'll see you after a while." She moves from child to child. "You want to be big like your daddy?"

"Yes..."

"Then go to sleep..."

Humming now, Clara Hale returns to the old rocker, carrying another baby. A small shaft of light is reflected in the mirror behind her. The chair begins to creak and sway. Mama Hale

Mama Hale rocks a young charge

bends down and kisses the baby's knuckles. The child wraps its tiny hand around Mrs. Hale's outstretched thumb and stares wide-eyed. Awake.

"Go to sleep . . ."

The humming begins again.

Mama Hale cannot recall a night without babies by her bed. She has been taking care of them since she was fourteen. Her voice is a soft whisper against the wind outside. There is no magic to what she does, just love, and that is the best magic of all.

"Sleep . . ."

Moonlight streams into a darkened room. Another town. Another night. A phone is ringing.

"Hello."

A short man, sitting in his underwear, slumps over a kitchen table. He is built like a welterweight boxer. In fact he was one.

"What?"

He grips the phone between his thumb and baby finger. The others prop up his head. He has the look of a fellow infected with the kind of tiredness sleep can't cure.

"Who is this?"

It is late.

"Yeah, you again."

His shoulder muscles tense. He shifts the receiver from one hand to the other and glances up at the window of his basement apartment.

"I'm not going to chase you, and I'm not going to watch you," he says in a rapid-fire delivery. "You're going to watch yourself." A long pause. "Okay?"

A muffled reply.

He looks up to the window again. He cannot see the moon from where he sits, but he hears the constant buzz of an overhead streetlight. A small wedge of brightness shines on the ceiling. Moonlight casts the rest of the room in blue, shimmering from dozens of trophies—long, silver lines of loving cups and footballs. The man holding the phone is a coach. He is talking to one of his boys.

"I've got enough confidence in you now to think that you'll do all right," the man says softly. "But if you don't, you're not failing me, you're failing yourself."

He is not talking football. He is talking drugs.

Calvin Woodland lives on a side of Washington we seldom see on the nightly news. It is far removed from the ruffles and flourishes of the nation's Capitol. Here survival is no global affair. Home is the grimy public housing projects southeast of the Capitol. Calvin Woodland's business is begging.

"How come you're always coming to me?" says the store owner, shuffling back from his counter the next morning. Calvin presses forward in a three-piece suit.

"How many times have I given to you last year?"

"Lots of times," says Woodland.

"And this year?" The owner moves to his cash register.

Calvin shrugs. Smiles. This is a ritual between friends.

"How much do you need?" says the owner.

"All you can stand."

For nearly two decades, Calvin Woodland has hustled these streets, raising money to help the drug addicts and dead-end kids who live in his neighborhood.

"Let me see your arm!" he shouts to a youngster who weaves through parked cars carrying a football. "Throw it!"

The boy ducks a pretend pass rush from a Volkswagen and lofts a high spiral down the sidewalk. Calvin leaps, plucking the ball from the path of an old lady pulling a grocery cart.

"Come on, Samson," he giggles. The boy smiles and falls in step.

Calvin Woodland represents something in short supply on these streets—a hero. He is coach of the Woodland Raiders, a pickup team of neighborhood kids that has not lost a football game in twelve years. Calvin is widely known in Washington, D.C., because of his ball players. Some go on to play college ball. One, Mike Martin, went all the way to the National Football League. But the coach plays a much more dangerous game off the field. Four years ago, he was shot in the knee trying to chase drug dealers from a street corner. He will do anything to keep his kids out of poisonous pastures.

"I help them survive," says Calvin as he pauses on his rounds. "I give them that meal. I give them a sweater. I go up somewhere and beg them a coat."

His players practice everyday. Everyday. Winter. Summer. Rain. Shine. They play anyone. But they must play by his rules. If they break the law, the coach will go to court with them; but he will not visit them in jail. If they are convicted, they must do their own time—alone.

"Tomorrow is the game!" Calvin pounds his fist. A four-year-old, sitting on the sideline, watches wide-eyed, peering out from an oversized helmet. Out on the practice field, his older brother faces the coach on bended knee. The coach looks out over his squad. They are dressed in a ragtag collection of uniforms. No one stirs.

"All day tomorrow, we've got business. Ya'll up to it?"

"Yes, sir!" they shout in unison.

"All you dope smokers, hide it tonight." Woodland stares into each face. Not an eye blinks.

"All you late beer drinkers, in the bed tonight." Calvin pauses and adds softly, "Okay?"

"Yes, sir!"

Calvin Woodland gave up a prizefighting career to help kids find dreams of their own. Over the years, he has taken twenty children into his home. His own youngsters have always shared their rooms with strangers. Until recently, he was rarely paid for his efforts. He was often out of work. Now Washington tax dollars provide him an $11,000 salary for a twenty-four-hour-a-day job.

Calvin Woodland's problems don't go home after five o'clock.

Each year, he throws a homecoming for all the boys who've passed his way. Coach Woodland does not remember the yards they gained. He knows who has a job. To Calvin Woodland, the most important contest is the game of life.

"We're not asking for any special favors," says the coach, placing his hand on a player's helmet. The team is huddled in prayer. "Only that You be with us. And we know we'll do the job..."

Calvin's message is simple: The world is a beautiful place. Some of the people in it are not. You may not be able to change what is bad, but you can get what you want and save what you get by working. You don't have to invest your life in a prison.

"I let them know that it won't be harsh all their life," says Calvin, sitting on the bench before kickoff. "If I prepare myself for winter, and I can hold out, I know that summer is coming. So, therefore, when times are hard and times are rough, if I can just hold out, I know the good times will be here soon."

"He's a great man," says Richard Clark, one of Calvin's former players, watching the game along the sidelines. "He's still doing the same old thing that he started out doing a long time ago. He sacrificed a lot to do it."

Clark would have been "Player of the Year" a few seasons back, but he skipped school. Calvin took the honor away. Today, Richard Clark is a medical technologist.

The crowd roars.

"Take it to the goal posts!" yells Clark as a Woodland Raider darts down the field. "Ha! Ha! Ha! He rolled like a big, ole bear. Way to go, champ!"

We watch a moment more, then I ask, "What does Calvin get out of this?"

Clark turns.

"He gets to show me off."

The Raiders were ahead 24–0 at half-time. By game's end, no one much looked at the scoreboard. Players, old and new, swarmed around Calvin.

"How long you plan to keep this up, Coach?" I shout through the swarm of clapping hands.

"I'll be here until the last kid is out of the ghetto."

Two players hoist him to their shoulders. "And then I'll find another ghetto."

The slapping and the happiness whirl down the field. Calvin bobs along the top.

"If you don't do nothin' else," he yells down to the faces beneath, "take some baths!"

The crowd dissolves in laughter.

On February 6, 1985, President Reagan introduced Clara Hale to Congress during his nationally televised State of the Union address. He called her "an American Heroine."

Supporters donated a van to haul the Woodland Raiders' equipment. The team decided to use it also to carry food. Ghetto kids now regularly feed the street people of Washington, D.C.

"*Stay Where You Are. I'll Come Find You*"

PHILADELPHIA, PENNSYLVANIA
(1981)

Remember all those stories about state mental hospitals a few years back? The hospitals were called "snake pits," warehouses where the sick and the insane were shipped and forgotten.

Those stories prompted many states to pass laws that cleared their mental health wards of all but the most dangerously ill. Other patients were expected to find help back in the community.

Well, life is a delicate balance. Those well-meaning reforms have created a whole new problem. Hundreds of thousands of mentally ill people, who are alone and poor and easily frightened, never found treatment outside the hospitals. They simply disappeared—out of sight, out of mind.

"I know that you don't want to go, and I know that you're frightened of the hospital."

A hand grips the telephone tightly. An ear listens to a voice in trouble.

"Stay where you are. I'll come find you."

Bill Eisenhuth cradles the receiver and heads for his car. For years he had listened to their calls. He wondered what became of them, the quiet ones who did not ask for help and never got better.

As a psychiatric aide in a Philadelphia hospital, Eisenhuth had watched patients come and go. Ten years ago, he followed them into the streets. His office became the steam vents and the alleys where his patients now live.

"Hi, Wilbur," says Eisenhuth to a man lying on the sidewalk. "I brought some coffee for you."

Each night between midnight and six, Bill Eisenhuth moves from man to man, carrying a kind word and a hamburger. It is an odyssey of trust.

"We made promises to these patients, and we never kept them," says Eisenhuth. "Now they're pretty well cut adrift and outside the system. For many patients, this is a subtle form of genocide. We sign their death warrant."

Police save whom they can, but emergency rooms and health clinics are so overloaded that there are few places for patients to go. They simply survive on heat vents and on handouts.

"How you feeling, Crawford?" Eisenhuth asks a man who sits in a swirl of steam.

"Poor," comes the reply.

Eisenhuth's patients are often mistaken for bums and winos. In fact, they are neither.

Crawford is so sick that he thinks the food Eisenhuth brought is poison and tosses it aside.

"I got a couple of dollars," says Eisenhuth, peering into a large cardboard box that is sitting on the sidewalk. "I'll give you a couple of dollars if you come out."

Frightened eyes blink back. There is no answer.

"That man has hidden inside that carton every night for six years," Eisenhuth says later. "There is a myth that these people are all old and ready to die. A lot of them are young. They're going to be this way for the rest of their lives."

Eisenhuth cannot make them well, but he can touch them. He is their companion on the dark side of night.

"One man certainly cannot make a difference to the total system," says Eisenhuth. "But, one man can make a difference in individual lives. And that's what I see, individual lives here."

Spending freely of his own time and money, Bill Eisenhuth does a job no one else wants. He sees twenty to forty men a night, and touches them all.

"Hello. Here's some food," says Eisenhuth to a man staring blankly at the stars. "Do you want it? Do you want me to leave it? How do you feel? Do you want a doctor?"

The man does not move.

"I'll stop by tomorrow."

"Does he have a name?" I ask.

"I've asked his name many times," says Eisenhuth. "He just looks at me and says, 'My name is No Name.'"

Border Angel

Forty years ago, a surveyor from Valentine, Nebraska, stood near here charting the land of the Rio Grande. He stopped for lunch and took a siesta. When he awoke, poor people had gathered to eat his scraps.

That bothered Frank Ferree. It bothered him so much he sold all his land and bought food and medicine for the poor. And when that money was gone, he begged for more, and people gave him more. He kept nothing for himself. For forty years, Frank Ferree has fed thousands on both sides of the Rio Grande.

I tell you this story because Frank Ferree is too modest. He rarely speaks. But what he has done is important. To do nothing is in every man's power.

"Here he comes!" shouts the crowd, and one thousand bodies push forward.

An old bus circles under the bridge, pulls up next to the people, and a big man begins passing out food. Victoria Gomez touches his hand. She has been standing in line for six hours. She is eighty-two. Alone. Deaf. She says Frank Ferree is all she has left.

"*La niña esta enferma,*" a mother says as she raises her little girl for the man to see. The baby's name is Maria Guadalupe. She has a blood disease. Frank Ferree found the doctors who keep her alive.

Every Saturday, Maria and her mother hitchhike from a distant ranch in Mexico to wait under the bridge near the border. United States and Mexican officials let Frank pass unhindered. Maria's mother worries about the day Frank will no longer come.

"All will be lost," she says.

Frank has been ill lately. A heart attack two years ago slowed his helping hands. Yet, at eighty-seven, he still comes. He is as constant as their need.

Francisco Godinez and his wife carry their baby between them on a blanket. Godinez is a construction worker, out of a job for nearly a year. His child has club feet. But the baby has no pain. Food is all they seek from Frank.

An old woman, her head covered with a black shawl, sits on the railroad tracks. Her name is Concepción Perez. She wants nothing. Frank once found a doctor to treat her daughter. So the old woman sits and sells pumpkinseeds each Saturday—just to be near him.

Friends keep Frank going. He gets no government aid, no charity donations. He does not belong to a church. He lives in a burned-out shack with four helpers, who have been at his side for twenty years. They exist on $481 a month, his military pension. They accept no more than they can give away each day.

"Does it bother you that you can't do more?" I ask.

"No," says Frank. "It appears that this is the only thing to do."

He lapses into silence, his eyes rheumy. The day's trek across the border has exhausted Frank Ferree. Aides have propped him up with pillows on the one chair in his home. They are busy restocking the bus for the next day's trip.

There is an awkward moment. I don't know whether to ask another question or to turn out the light and leave him alone. Ferree looks to the window. Something in the yard stirs him to speak. His voice is barely a whisper.

"I walked for several years with a knapsack of penicillin, making deliveries in Matamoros and Reynosa, border towns. That was before we got the bus. You do what you can."

I touch his arm. "What is your dream?"

Another silence. The bus doors slam outside.

"What is your . . ."

"What's that?" says the old man, leaning forward.

"What is your dream?" I repeat.

Frank Ferree lifts a big, rawboned hand and waves it near his face. He looks like Abe Lincoln grown old.

"Nothing," he says absently. "No more. Today. Today. Tomorrow will be tomorrow."

Friends tried to help Frank build a new clinic, but he gave the building supplies to the poor. He has been honored many times. Twice nominated for a Nobel Prize. Five presidents of Mexico have given him gold medals. He melted down the medals and bought beans.

Mobile Doctor

Growing up, I was in and out of doctors' offices a lot—part of the last wave of polio victims. I remember that almost every office had a Norman Rockwell picture on the wall of a kindly old country doctor who took the time to treat a little girl's doll.

I got to thinking the other day that those same medical miracles that cured things like my polio also took their toll on doctors' time, made them more remote, put them in high-rise offices where they could be close to their life-giving machines.

We've got better medicine now, but perhaps something personal has been lost along the way. There's a physician in Fort Lauderdale, Florida, who's trying to bring back that personal touch.

"Harder, harder, breathe harder!" says Dr. Jim Andersen. His patient, Nick Venezia, looks as though he has tasted thunder. Venezia has come to Dr. Andersen, frightened by the first long breath of age. He didn't have far to go. The doctor drove the office to him.

"I get less for a house call than an air-conditioning man," says Andersen, stepping into the truck that pulls his clinic around the neighborhood.

"If a patient doesn't drive, if he has to go even five miles to a doctor's office, it's sometimes a big stumbling block, so they don't go. So it's a simple matter. If you can't have the patient come to the medicine, you take the medicine to the people."

Four days a week, Doc Andersen makes his appointed rounds. The fifth day is set aside for repairs. He does his own work on the mobile clinic to keep patient fees low.

"I bought this whole rig, the office, all the equipment in it, and the truck to pull it," says Andersen, "for less than most physicians spend a year on their office lease."

His nurse, Eileen Barney, runs the clinic from a pay phone.

"Hi, Steve. This is Eileen. It's okay to refill the Dyazide."

Emergency cases are sent to the hospital, but Andersen has kept Bob Carey alive and at home because the doctor also makes house calls.

"Can you show us the bleeding?" says Andersen.

Carey leans against a sink. He has emphysema. He is attached to a respirator by a long plastic hose. The tube connection has rubbed his neck raw. Andersen locates the problem and stops the bleeding.

"How are you on supplies?" he asks, repacking his bag.

"I'm okay, Doc. Thanks."

Out on the sidewalk, a neighbor calls across his yard, "Doctor Livingstone, I presume?"

Three men look up from their lawn mowers and laugh. Andersen smiles.

"How are you, Doctor?"

"Good," says Andersen.

"You're looking well," says the neighbor. "How do you feel?"

"I feel fine," says Andersen. "What's that you got in your hand?"

"Oh, that." The neighbor flicks away a cigarette.

"He's always smoking," says the neighbor's wife, who has come to the door to see whom her husband is talking to. "What are you going to do? If you keep walking around and catching him, maybe he'll stop."

Andersen is the conscience of the community.

"I keep trying to stop," says the neighbor.

"He promised," says the wife. "He promised that's he going to slow up."

"I'll check back," says Andersen.

At first, there was some reluctance to trust a doctor whose office looked like a bookmobile.

"The first time I saw Doc's clinic bouncing down the road," says the neighbor, "I wondered if it was worthwhile to try a doctor like that. Was he going to be there for one week, and then we won't see him again? But he hasn't pulled the trailer away yet and not pulled it back."

Doc Andersen's waiting room is full at each stop.

"He talks to you," says a patient. "You know, if you want to talk to him, he waits. A lot of doctors don't do that."

Outside the trailer, the sun is setting.

"I'll call you Jim, okay?" says the patient.

"That's what my mother calls me," says Andersen, with a gentle smile.

"Look, Doctor," says the man. "I eat like a fool when I give up cigarettes."

"Well," says Andersen, checking the man's ample stomach, "it doesn't look like you've been doing too bad *with* the cigarettes."

It is nighttime now, fourteen hours after Andersen first started his rounds. The lights go on inside the clinic.

There's still work to be done.

"People haven't changed that much," says Andersen. "Feelings haven't changed that much. Families are still families."

Some doctors haven't changed that much either.

"Angels on the Roof"

There comes a time when our friends and families expect us to
retire. Relax. Finish what we've been doing all our lives. Places
like this Florida beach are the dream, the reward for some. Endless weeks under a gold-coin sun. But for most of us, the days
come down empty—with no riches, just memories.

"Oh, oh, here come my trouble." Rachel Johnson scurries
from house to house, tossing newspapers into her car. Neighbors
have stacked them on their porches for Rachel to pick up and
sell at a recycling center. She is one step ahead of the garbage
men, who are making their rounds. "Hey, how ya'll this morning?" She makes a living on what they come to throw away.
"They take everything that isn't nailed down," she says in
disgust. It is a daily ritual, this race with the garbage men. Rachel
Johnson is seventy-two.

Six years ago, her doctor told her to stop cleaning other
people's homes. The work was becoming too strenuous for her
weak heart. "When the dirt gets so high you can't step over it,"
he had said, "you'll have to walk around it."

She's been walking ever since.

Rachel and her neighborhood have grown old together. Porches are rotting. Roofs leak. There is not much money or muscle to fix them.

"One night I was in the bed, and it was storming," she says. "The water came right down through the light fixtures. That was what waked me up. That hot water pouring on my feet."

The morning after that leak, Rachel Johnson heard about an extraordinary group of women, middle-aged, divorced house-wives whose homes had also fallen into disrepair. The women had banded together to teach each other construction skills. They stayed together to help senior citizens in need. They are down the street this morning repairing Lee Holden's home.

"Where can I walk?" asks construction foreman Angela Martinez. She is dressed in a red tee shirt and jeans held up by a carpenter's belt filled with tools. Mr. Holden's kitchen rug is stretched like a tarpaulin. Angela Martinez tests it with her toe. She rips back the carpet. There is no floor underneath.

"Oh, my goodness!" It is said with a schoolteacher's dis-approval. "My goodness!" Angela Martinez leans over, clinging to the doorframe, to inspect the hole beneath. "Watch out for the mice, Frances."

Frances Potts and the three other women on the crew slide into the hole and begin to build the new floor. Lee Holden will not have to pay for this repair because Angela Martinez has persuaded a local business to underwrite the cost. In effect, busi-nesses in Tampa "adopt" older folk's dilapidated homes and pay the all-female crew to fix them.

Carolyn Stahl looks up from her sander and wipes a smear of dirt onto her face.

"I think when you feel that everything is falling apart in your own life"—she clicks off her machine to make her point—"you want to restructure things in the lives of others."

She steadies the stove, which is perched on a piece of rotten two-by-four, then continues. "I just couldn't stand seeing things falling apart anymore. It was a very emotional thing for me."

In three years, Carolyn and the others have made three hundred emergency repairs. The women had not worked construction before their divorces. They learned on the job, gradually taking on larger projects.

They learned quickly and grew to be so highly regarded in Tampa that one year they went commercial. But it wasn't the same as working for the elderly.

"It was exciting at first to get paid so well, but then it was just another job," says Angela, smiling at Mr. Holden. "We missed the hugs and the love. They made the sore backs, black fingers, and smashed toes worth it."

This crew doesn't just fix homes. It patches up people's lives.

"Oh, here comes the door!" Jackie Caravella claps her hands and stares in amazement. Her neat gray hair is piled tightly upon her head, which she shakes now from side to side. She reminds you of Tweetie Bird's aunt. If bustles were in fashion, she'd wear one.

Mrs. Caravella lost her husband of fifty years the summer before. He was an artist. Angela put a window in her new backdoor so she would have more light to see his paintings.

"It's very nice," says Mrs. Caravella, gathering the construction crew to her. "Very nice. Oh, I appreciate it." She hugs them all. "I love that window."

Their truck rumbles off. It has been a long day, but there is one last stop—Rachel Johnson's house. Frances and Angela scamper up a ladder, locate the leak, and begin to slather tar. It takes longer than expected.

"I think you need a little bit more butter in your batter," chides Angela, as the goo begins to thicken in the bucket. "Maybe we didn't whip it long enough." She grins and slaps a shingle. "It's just like frosting a cake!"

An old man, watching the goings-on from his yard swing, catches my attention. "You'll never guess what Rachel has on her house," he says, his foot hitting the worn spot in the grass beneath his glider. It creaks to a stop. "Angels on her roof."

Ruby Walker

MUSKOGEE, OKLAHOMA

(1979)

Most everybody in Muskogee knows Ruby Walker. She is an inexhaustible wisp of a woman who cleans twenty-seven houses a week, five houses a day, two on Saturdays. It has been her routine for twenty years, since her husband died.

Most are big homes, as you might expect. But Ruby also works the other side of town. Folks there need more than her dusting and cleaning. They need her friendship.

One of Ruby's special clients was a retired painter who had a thirst for booze and a chronic heart disease. For six dollars a week, Ruby cleaned his home, did his laundry, took him to the doctor, even drove him to Texas to visit old friends. And when he died, she buried him.

"When I first met him," says Ruby, "he just had an old footlocker, not many clothes or nothing. He moved three or four different times, and I moved him 'cause he didn't have no family or nobody to see about him. I just started helping him."

When he died, he left all he had to Ruby—the old house she had cleaned so often and $10,000 he had quietly saved for her from his veteran's pension.

Ruby rented the house to a working mother. She has never touched the $10,000. You see, Ruby already has a home, the same one she and her husband moved into thirty-seven years ago. And her garden is full, with plenty of pumpkins and potatoes for fresh-baked pies and winter canning. Plenty for which to be thankful.

"I work for so many people that's sick and crippled and invalid, cancer and everything," says Ruby, "I figure I got all I need."

Ruby's tiny home is filled with clothes. She washes them for folks in her spare time. And, from time to time, they give her some discarded hand-me-downs. Most, she passes on to others who have none.

On Sundays, when her church gathers for a prayer breakfast, Ruby works alone in the church kitchen, cleaning up. But she is not alone. She has surrounded herself with people who need her. She has reaped a rich harvest—faith, food, friends, and health—a harvest of happiness she plants every day of the year.

Jimmy's Kids

CARROLLTON, TEXAS
(1982)

We talk a lot about sports legends. Legend is a word we use easily. A team wins thirteen games—legendary. A guy tosses one good season of baseball—he's a legend. A single Saturday afternoon thrill—legendary.

But what of the legends who build quietly, year in and year out, until they touch us all. They are the most unusual sportsmen.

Jimmy Porter has spent most of his nights under the lights of the baseball diamonds of north Texas. For sixty summers, he has gently coaxed the kids of Carrollton, Texas, to play the game he loves.

"Hi, Jimmy," says a father, holding his three-year-old son by the hand. "This is Jason."

Jimmy flicks his eyes to the boy.

"This is my little boy," says the father.

"How you doing?" says Jimmy.

"Say 'Hi, Jimmy.'"

"Hi, Jimmy." The little boy's words are hidden behind the knuckles in his mouth.

"Jimmy taught me baseball," says the father. "You wanna learn how to play baseball from Jimmy?"

The boy's face brightens.

Kids flock to Jimmy like ants to a picnic. He is a pied piper, seldom more than a pebble kick from the nearest ball park.

He lives alone. He has never married. But he knew what he wanted a long time ago. Jimmy built his life around the kids. For forty years he lived in a boxcar to be near their ball park. When the boxcar was moved, he built a shack. When the shack was torn down, he found a house nearby. It is stuffed with clippings and gifts from the kids he has coached.

"Some people say, 'Jimmy, you're poor.' But I say, 'I've been poor long enough to get used to it!'" He rolls his head back in a hearty laugh. "I just love baseball and I love the kids. I get so much kick out of playing with them."

Jimmy Porter is eighty-one, one of the few who remain from that generation of innocents for whom a game is still a game and not a bottom line. His life each year begins with the first warm days of summer when the kids return to where he has never left.

"When you get up here and start batting," says Jimmy, snapping his wrist to show a young ball player how to swat at a pitch, "don't go down, stand up straight."

The child listens. Jimmy is a sports legend in Carrollton. Not because he had once played in the old Negro Leagues with Satchel Paige, which he did, but because he got homesick for the kids, and gave it all up.

"Pow!" yells Jimmy. "The ball bounced off my bat and knocked that pitcher out. The umpire said, 'You hit him!' I said, 'I didn't hit him!' He said, 'You hit him!' I said, 'No, I didn't. I hit the ball. The ball hit him.'"

Jimmy and the children laugh together.

The Little League game begins. Jimmy walks to his frayed folding chair behind the screen at home plate. A small boy touches Jimmy's shoulder as the old man turns to sit.

Jimmy Porter smiles for the camera

"You used to give out autographs, didn't you?" says the boy.

"Yeah," says Jimmy.

Carrollton, Texas, named a park after Jimmy, but he seldom goes there. It's too far. You'll find him where the kids are.

"Jimmy," says the small boy.

"Hum?" says Jimmy.

"I'm going to try to come out to your house sometime this week." The boy has a hopeful look. "Maybe me and you can play some baseball."

The Turtle Lady

Padre Island is a tiny finger of land that points ninety miles down the gulf coast of Texas. Few people live there. Mostly it's just sand dunes and seagulls—and a woman who can talk to turtles.

"Now don't you worry," says the old woman, climbing the sand dune. "There'll be plenty of food and plenty of other little turtles to play with."

The baby squirms in her arms.

"Sweetheart, put your little head down."

The old woman's name is Illa Loetscher. Most folks just call her the Turtle Lady.

For twenty years, Illa Loetscher has opened her home to the sick and wounded—turtles tossed up on the shore and left to die. She gives them the kind of care only a mother would give. Most get well.

At age seventy-four, Mrs. Loetscher attempted an evolutionary miracle. The Mexican government gave her a very special turtle to see if she could raise it, send it to sea, and have it return to her. It did.

The turtle was a kemp's ridley, the most endangered sea turtle in the world. The few ridleys that remain lay most of their eggs on Mexican beaches where, for years, those eggs have been stolen and eaten as a love potion. Mexican and American authorities would like some of the ridleys to lay their eggs farther north, in Texas, away from danger.

"This is Jonathan Livingston Sea Turtle," says Mrs. Loetscher to a small group of children sitting in her living room. The turtle is wearing a sweater and a hat.

Illa Loetscher and Geraldine

Mrs. Loetscher is putting on a show to recruit neighborhood kids to help her find the endangered animals.

"This is Geraldine."

The youngsters giggle at a turtle wearing a nightgown.

"She is four years old."

She is also one of those rare ridleys saved by a father whose child had been to the Turtle Lady's house.

Mrs. Loetscher names each turtle after the person who found it.

"The children feel that these are real little people," says Mrs. Loetscher, "and so do I. To me, Geraldine is a real live little girl."

She leans over and kisses the turtle's nose.

"And I'm always going to keep her that way."

"And when you say good-bye to Geraldine?" I ask softly.

"Oh, I'm not thinking of that. I'm just living in happiness now. But, someday, we'll have to let her go."

Those "somedays" come all too often. Mrs. Loetscher wades into the surf. The tiny turtle slips from her hand.

"Bye-bye, hon," she says.

One by one, Mrs. Loetscher returns her "children" to the sea.

"Bye-bye, baby."

If she is successful and the ridley comes back to Texas to lay her eggs, Illa Loetscher will be the happiest mom in America.

"Oh, there she goes, there goes my baby. Bye-bye, baby. Bye-bye."

FOUR

A Sense of Place

"*I've et so many eggs,
I can't look at the rear end of a chicken.*"
NEWT KEEN

Two Families

(1984)

Come on. Take an early morning walk with me. I want you to
meet a family, Jim and Marty Dwyer and their five boys. That's
their son, Chris, delivering papers.

The Dwyers always wanted a baby girl but figured it wasn't
going to happen after those five boys. So they agreed to raise
someone else's. But she wasn't a baby. And she brought her
brother. And those two brought four more.

"What is this?" A young Vietnamese, one of many crowded
around the supper table, is teasing a towheaded boy sitting next
to him.

"Spaghetti," says the towhead. "It's just like long rice."

The two begin to laugh. Laughter spreads from place to place
as the spaghetti bowl is passed. When it reaches Jim Dwyer, he
adds this observation.

"Never sit near the baby." It is spoken with the sure knowledge of a man who's been married twenty-two years. He tucks in his napkin and repeats. "Never sit near the baby. You got to feed him."

The accent is Long Island, New York, where Jim and Marty Dwyer met and lived before they moved West. They wanted to own a horse ranch, but they run a muffler shop instead. Their dream changed four years ago when they agreed to look after an entire additional family. There are fourteen of them now. The new faces around this supper table came two at a time from Vietnam, drifting in from the calm surface of an endless sea.

"After the Communists took over, my dad lost his job," Thu-Nga explains. She is the youngest Vietnamese, just sixteen, a slight girl with a cherub's face. She looks much younger, doll-like. "The whole family tried to escape together many times." She pauses. "We couldn't make it." Her eyes begin to glisten. "By law in Vietnam, if you leave your home without permission, they take your house. My mom and dad decided that we had to split up."

Two by two, her father, Tran Van Be, sent his children to freedom. They slipped away in the night down to the ocean.

"Our boat was just a tiny wooden one," Thu-Nga says, "about sixteen-foot long by seven-foot wide. It was built for three people. We had three hundred twenty-three people on it. The first day we went out, the engine broke, so we couldn't go anywhere. We found out that we didn't have a pilot. We didn't have any food. Water was in every direction, but you couldn't drink it."

She and her sister, Thu-Van, almost gave up.

"We were just waiting to die, but we didn't know if death would come soon or the next wave would send us to the bottom. We saw many ships pass by, but none would stop for us. By the seventh evening, we spotted an American ship. It stopped and picked us up."

Marty Dwyer pulls some spaghetti sauce off the stove and continues the story.

"I remember Thu-Hong was standing right here when she got

the telegram that her sisters had escaped. I almost had to peel her off the ceiling, she jumped so high. Just one incredible leap!"

Thu-Nga's parents still live in Saigon (now Ho Chi Minh City) with their youngest son and a daughter who tried to escape but was turned back. She and her sixteen-month-old baby were in one boat. Her husband, Xuong, was forced into another. Xuong made it to America and now lives near the Dwyers. He has not seen his wife and child in three years.

A big chestnut stallion lopes down the mountain. "Here comes Hopalong Xuong!" The family, gathered in the foothills, watches Xuong's approach.

"Go get 'em Xuong! Atta boy!" He is holding on with his knees. The stirrups flop freely beneath his sneakers.

"How do I stop him?"

"Pull back on the reins!" shouts Jim.

The family is on an outing, horseback riding in the Rocky Mountain foothills.

"Eeeeek! Wait a minute! Help! Wait!" Thu-Van screams. Her horse has ambled over to some grass and lowers its head. Thu-Van is frantically holding on to the pommel to keep from sliding down its neck.

"Come on, you rode elephants," Jim says playfully. "You can ride a horse."

He reaches for the reins and settles Thu-Van back into the saddle, then prods the horse on its way. "See you next week."

"Oh, noooo, Dad . . ."

This is as close as Jim Dwyer has gotten to his dream of owning a ranch.

"If five more [Vietnamese] came tomorrow, well, we'd just postpone it again." He is watching his children romping across the meadow. "I don't think that was much of a decision, to tell you the truth."

Jim works thirteen-hour days, six days a week, at the muffler shop—surrounded by his boys.

"We try to give our children everything they need," he says, taking a break behind the cash register, later that day. He looks through the glass divider that separates the office from the garage area. Two sons are changing a tire. Another is welding. Shards of blue light break upon his face. "We give them everything they need," Jim repeats softly, as if he has just thought of it, "but they have to earn what they want."

His son Brian works two jobs. He leaves the shop on Friday nights and delivers newspapers until dawn. His son Chris tosses them through the week. Chris took the job when the Vietnamese first came, to raise money for college. He had just turned ten.

"When I get mad," says Chris, flipping a newspaper from the back of his mother's station wagon, "sometimes, you feel like, 'Oh, it's their fault.' " Another house. Another flick of the wrist. He is a good shot. The paper flops on the porch. "But that's just because you're mad," he laughs to himself. "When you stop to think it over, it's not their fault."

Marty Dwyer was set to study nursing when the Vietnamese arrived. She had to cancel her enrollment. That evening in the kitchen, I asked her if she ever regretted that decision to take the Vietnamese in.

"Of course, of course, we've all said, 'What am I, crazy? I'm broke! Get out everybody. I'm going to go wild at the Fashion Bar!' " Two kids look around the corner. She smiles. Her voice trails away. "We just can't do that . . ."

The older children all go to college. Thu-Nga plans to study medicine at Johns Hopkins. She is a straight "A" student.

"Every time we see them accomplish something, we think of what they [the Vietnamese parents] are missing," says Jim waiting in the living room for dinner. "Yeah, we think about them a lot. I think they're very special. I wouldn't be in their shoes for anything."

Marty wanders in as their youngest son sets the table. The three of us watch him for a moment, and then I say, "You and

Jim couldn't imagine having to sit at a table and decide some night how to send your kids out to a better life."

It was not a question, just a statement.

"I don't think I could love enough to give them up like that," she says, her eyes moist. "You must love your kids an incredible amount to let them risk their lives."

"He's got three more children there," Jim reminds us. "Imagine what they [he and his wife] are going through as they wonder, 'Should we let these go or should we not? Then we'll have no children here.' "

Thu-Nga joins us on the sofa. "My mom would say, 'Yes, let them go,' and my dad would say, 'No.' The next day my dad would say, 'Yes,' and my mom would say, 'No.' They just didn't have any idea where we would go, to which country or anything."

"The guy must really love his children to do that," says Jim. "He passed on his own personal happiness to better his children. I guess that's the ultimate in parenthood."

Tran Van Be is allowed to write to his family but can say little. Letters are censored and take months to travel back and forth. Last year he sent Thu-Nga the ancient, oriental Dan Tranh, a stringed instrument she once played. On its side, inlaid with abalone shells, is the history of Vietnam. He did not want her to forget.

His oldest child, Thu-Van, wants to marry. Jim and Tran Van Be are coordinating the wedding plans. The Dwyers have petitioned the Vietnamese government to let her natural parents join them.

"That'll be a day." Marty shakes her head. "Boy, I don't know if the sun will go down that day."

"What was the last thing your mom and dad told you before you left?" I asked Thu-Nga.

"We had dinner together for the last time. My mom had kept me home from school that day because those were our last hours together." Thu-Nga looks off, remembering. "And, so . . ." She stifles her sadness by grinning as hard as she can. "We had dinner together, and we prayed together. And . . ." Again she glances away. On the wall there is a photograph of her mother and father in Saigon, surrounded, in happier times, by children. It is the only picture she has of them. Thu-Nga smiles, but her eyes are full of tears. "She said that if we ever make it to America, just do our best." Tears roll down her cheeks. She swallows, "Well, they just said they have a lot of hope for us. And they have high hope for us. That we should try to reach it."

"Where's Thu-Nga?" A voice from the other room. Kids crowd around the table.

"She's coming . . ."

A family is made up of stories about itself. This family is an anthology of us all.

A Last Reprieve

The sea islands that lace the Georgia and South Carolina coasts number in the hundreds. But the sun rises and the surf flames over only one, still separate, secure, timeless. The Spanish called it Santa Catalina de Guale.

On this pine-dense Atlantic island thirty miles south of Savannah, there are beaches unspoiled since sailors first marked them in the sixteenth century. Gnats play hide-and-seek in the sunbeams. There are no telephones, no bridges—just wild, savage loneliness.

St. Catherines Island is the last of the great barrier isles untouched by government or real estate development. Here there are Indian graves undisturbed for four thousand years.

A fellow by the name of Button Gwinnett built the first house on this island. His signature is on the Declaration of Independence. His old home later served as the capitol for what was to become an all-black state. The house still stands.

For nearly a century, the place was a rich man's playground, last owned by Edward J. Noble, the fellow who made millions by punching little holes in candy and calling them Life Savers.

Today his island is saving life itself. St. Catherines is a remote sanctuary for the vanishing animals of the world. John Woods watches over them.

"You don't have to worry about sleeping late," says Woods.

It was a few moments past dawn, and each animal was blasting forth with its best Janis Joplin imitation. The noise was deafening.

"I think it would be tough for me to come back to the twentieth century," he says with a grin.

For forty years, Woods and his family have been caretakers of this paradise, living alone with only an occasional visitor.

Seven years ago, a herd of African gemsbok came to share their Eden. Noble had died. His daughter had interested the Bronx Zoo in taking on the island as an experiment. St. Catherines would become a remote sanctuary for endangered species and, for some, perhaps a last reprieve from extinction.

"You have to be selective," says John Lucas, the research director for the project. "You're not going to be able to save all the animals."

But the gemsbok flourished. Soon, Dama gazelle arrived from Senegal, hartebeest from Uganda, and addax from the Sahara. Threatened species were shipped from all over to loll under St. Catherines' safe sun.

The preserve specializes in hooved animals and a few rare birds. They are constantly tended and carefully bred. Scientists teach reluctant parents how to impress their mates. I watch as Al Venzuella approaches a waddled crane, a huge bird, nearly half his size. The bird lets him stroke her wings, then hops away like a young girl trying to run on stilts. That's a waddled crane's version of "not tonight, honey, I've got a headache."

When necessary, researchers and their families do the baby-sitting so mothers can have more offspring. Some animals have eight times as many there as they do in the wild.

In short, St. Catherines is a bank. Animals are deposited, their numbers increase, and the investment is returned to nature.

Some developing nations were slow to accept this at first.

"They were just so busy trying to survive," says Lucas, "they couldn't understand why somebody would come three, four, five thousand miles to look at a giraffe or a zebra when the darn things just get in your way."

A Pesquet's parrot interrupts his thoughts, sounding like a car battery on a cold morning. When the noise grinds down, Lucas continues.

"The Arabian countries were very poor, you know, sixty or seventy years ago. And now they're some of the richest countries. They're looking for Arabian oryx that were once found in the deserts of Saudi Arabia. They don't have any left. They were shot out, lost, and are now nearly extinct. Now the Arabian countries want more, and they're lucky we have some."

There were only sixteen Arabian oryx left in the world a few years back. Now there are three thousand. Scientists are experimenting with embryo transplants to see if surrogate mothers could possibly carry oryx babies. The embryo would be placed in a gemsbok for a time, then the oryx mother would be re-impregnated, doubling the number of young she could normally bear in a season.

"I think the program is worthwhile because the animals you see are very beautiful, and people have a justified right to see these animals. Even in captivity, they're better than a stuffed animal in a museum."

Behind us cranes and macaws clamor for their breakfast, like the spoiled children they are. Lucas excuses himself. John Woods and I go for a drive. This is not a zoo with cameras or crowds. Only scientists and an occasional guest are allowed on the island.

"There's a rare white oak," says Woods as our truck bounces down a dirt road. "We have very few of those."

We pull into a thick underbrush of cane and palmettos.

"This is a beautiful spot here. I made this into a picnic area, and this is where I keep my boat. Right down there."

He stops the truck. We go for a walk. Woods tells me he left the island at one time in his life to work on the mainland but returned to take the caretaker's job when his father retired.

"I was doing very well where I was," he says, resting on a stump. "I was making two or three hundred dollars a week." He slaps at a mosquito but misses, the mosquito doesn't. "And I came over here for three hundred dollars a month. Worked two or three years for that price."

Woods stares across the water at the Georgia coast.

"It's nice to go to the mountains," he sighs. "It's nice to go to the city for three or four days, but I'm always glad to get back."

A deer jumped in front of our jeep.

"Late in the afternoon, you see a lot of 'em," Woods points out. "There goes another one. Two more. Another. You just don't see deer like that on these other islands."

St. Catherines has so far escaped the conflicting current of our times. But it, too, is the last of its kind—an endangered species, like the animals it folds into itself.

Daufuskie Island, about thirty-five miles north of St. Catherines, is a little piece of sand and trees near Savannah. A thousand people once lived there, until the oyster beds died and the forest grew back. Now, there are only eighty-five.

Life changes slowly. There are no paved roads, no street lights, no bridge to the outside. It is quiet here, too. The only excitement on Daufuskie is an occasional alligator swimming deeply through the miles of marshland or a rambunctious razor-back hog. I suppose there are some who would say the island is too quiet. We have been led to believe that life is happiest when we are entertained. Well, that is a luxury of modern times. Time was when boredom was not such a bad thing. It built imagination and wrote a lot of books.

Daufuskie Island, South Carolina, is a place so remote, the mind can be your best friend.

Only the very old and the very young live here. Teenagers

must move to the mainland to finish their education. Most of the parents work there, too. The island's elementary school has eleven children.

One winter they put together a magazine of their thoughts. Not so unusual, really, except that the publisher, Shannon Wilkinson, who was working on a grant from the South Carolina Arts Commission, printed eight hundred copies by mistake. All eight hundred were sold by word of mouth, nationwide, in less than ten weeks.

Life on Daufuskie gives children time to think and to feel. There is something of the poet in this school.

Here is what eleven-year-old Jennifer Smith wrote:

> Tears are like stars
> coming out of your eyes.

And Donald Jenkins, age twelve:

> Smiles are like music
> without noise.

The children of Daufuskie

And Darrell King, age thirteen:

> Disgust is like
> a wild jungle beast
> taking leadership
> of your emotions . . .

Tonya Robinson, age nine:

> Tears are like little
> drips of rocks . . .

The genius of this country is almost always in its kids, who see things as they really are and dream dreams as if they were new.

> Suppose you were walking
> down the road . . .
> And a tree said,
> "Come climb me."
>
> Try to be a bald eagle
> who can see
> around the world.
>
> Try to be a rocket
> with bird wings.
> Try to be a moon
> with no glow.

That came from Alberto Stevens and Donald Jenkins, both twelve. They had help from Larry Forrest and his friend, Bobby Stevens, just eleven.

> If I was the sky
> I would let the birds
> fly in me.
> I would have
> clouds for friends.
> The sun
> would be my neighbor . . .

So wrote Donald Jenkins. And Jennifer's sister, Michelle, age ten, answered:

> Try to imagine you are a
> cloud in the shape of a
> rabbit, eating treetops
> and hopping over
> rainbows . . .

Their teachers, Carol and Jim Alberto, say the children on Daufuskie are not all that different from other kids. All children have potential. They just don't always draw upon it. Their time is cut in tiny slices, too thin for thought.

"I like it over here on Daufuskie," says Darrell King, "because there are no signs and people don't go to jail. It doesn't have many cars and not any police."

"Daufuskie is very little," Bobby Stevens points out. And then he adds. "There are no crazy people on Daufuskie."

Money from the sale of the magazine is going into a scholarship fund so what has been thought will not be lost.

Larry Forrest, eleven:

> Smiles remind me of
> hamburgers
> because they are
> big . . .

Life will soon change here. Developers are buying up land. They want to build a resort similar to nearby Hilton Head Island. The Albertos worry about what awaits these youngsters when the outside world comes calling. The children are thinking about that too.

Jonathan Wiley:

> Try to stop a train with
> one hand.

Loving County

When all the political reporters are out tailing behind candidates, sampling the mood of America, I like to come back to Loving County, Texas. There are no media events out here. I've never been too comfortable with what a man tells me when a brass band is playing.

No, Loving County is important to me because folks out here never forgot how to take care of themselves. They have to. This is the most sparsely populated county in the country, 647 square miles of nothing but sagebrush, rattlesnakes, and sand. There is a town in Loving, but it is so remote that folks have to haul their drinking water for forty miles.

County judge, Don Creager, jokes that the population is not likely to boom.

"Every time a baby is born," says Creager, "some man leaves town."

Still, there are some benefits. The county's one tennis court is hardly ever crowded. And with Sheriff Punk Jones on the job, there is very little crime. Oil and gas rigs provide plenty of work for the 110 people who want to live there. No one is unemployed, no one is on welfare.

Each month, Judge Creager tries to explain all this to dozens of federal agencies that send him questionnaires.

"I'm trying to cut out the bureaucracy," says Creager.

On the bottom of each form he writes, "Unemployment, zero; welfare, zero. We don't want your money!"

But not everyone in Washington believes him. One year, the Labor Department counted the seventeen school children in Loving County and announced there was 17 percent unemployment—so much unemployment that county businesses were eligible for preferential treatment on federal contracts. There are only two businesses.

Newt Keen figured he didn't need federal money to sell hamburgers. He runs the only cafe in Loving County. The house specialty is fifty-cent beer and raw eggs.

"I've et so many eggs," says Newt, "I can't look at the rear end of a chicken."

Mattie Thorpe, a grandmother, runs the other business in Loving. She pumps gas into all fifty-six cars in the county. She doesn't want more. Her work already interrupts her knitting more than she'd like.

Judge Creager wrote a two-line reply to the Labor Department.

"Who do you think would live out here if he didn't have a job? There is *no* unemployment."

The government decided to get tough. A letter arrived demanding that Loving County integrate its grade school and set up a music program.

"There were only two kids in the school," says Creager, "and one of them is tone deaf. Both were white."

The judge wrote back and said, "We can't."

A telegram came singing across the wires: "You must integrate your faculty."

Creager went sixty miles looking for a black teacher. He found one, but the man didn't want to come. Creager told the government that, and back came a note saying that federal aid would now be cut off.

Well, Loving County wasn't getting any federal aid. It never had. The only federal money in town was the post office. Washington spent sixty-five dollars a month to handle three dozen letters a day—most of them junk mail.

Edna Dewise, the county clerk, thinks all this is a waste.

"When you take your tax money from here," says Edna, "and it goes to Washington, and then filters out into the various departments, and finally dribbles back, you've lost 50 percent of your money."

There was one check that the people of Loving County couldn't get Washington to take back, a two-thousand-dollar anti-recession payment. It sat on Creager's desk for a month. The townspeople finally used it to buy some extra sleep in the morning. They put up an automatic flagpole. It works with the sun on an electric eye. Each evening, the whole town meets over at Newt Keen's cafe to place bets on what time the flag will go down.

So, there you have it, Washington. One town that doesn't need help. It can pull its own strings—automatically.

Basque Sheepherder

BUTTE VALLEY, NEVADA
(1981)

Some folks say we have lost our sense of place. People have little time for where they are. The future lies over the mountain out on the four-lane. Well, that's not so unusual really. America was built by a nation of nomads.

One man who settled in Butte Valley, Nevada, never stopped moving. For ninety-three years, he has carried his home in his heart.

You find Beltran Paris by listening for the wind chimes, thousands of sheep's bells ringing their way to water. He is almost always behind this moving white blanket of sheep, high in the mountains of eastern Nevada. For most of this century, Beltran Paris has walked his animals to winter quarters 150 miles in the desert below. It is a hard and lonely life, set to the rhythm of the sheep. He has kept at it because he has a dream.

"I look for tomorrow," says Beltran. "I look for tomorrow, today."

In all those hours alone, Beltran Paris had set a plan. He would take his pay in sheep. One day, his children and his children's children would live in the valley he walked.

From his tiny herd has grown a seven-thousand-acre ranch, with cattle as well as sheep. His sons and his grandsons all have homes beneath the towering buttes.

Beltran Paris is one of the last of the old-time mountain men who came from France and Spain to take a job few people wanted. Most of the Basques worked hard and then went home. In Nevada's vast mountains, there was no neighborhood to ease the loneliness of the new land. The shepherds scratched notes to each other in the aspens.

"We used to cut letters into the skin of the trees," says Beltran, "and as the skin grew and the trees got bigger, it raised the letters so our friends could read."

The notes were a comforting "hello" to those who followed and felt alone.

There were two million sheep in Nevada when Beltran Paris came to America. Now there are fewer than one hundred thousand. The work is hard and constant, and costs are high. But for a man with a dream, there is consolation. Beltran's sons, their children and his great-grandchildren all sit at the same dinner table each evening. Beltran Paris is ninety-three. His table is the yearbook of his life. A life his sons no longer recommend to their sons.

"We enjoy our work," says Pete Paris. "I don't mind working from daylight 'til dark. That don't really bother me. But the fact that you really haven't gained much. You'd think after working forty years, maybe you could sit back and tell somebody else to do it. You know what I mean. After forty years, it looks like you could."

Pete Paris glanced at his father and smiled.

"But then, he's been at it for eighty years, so I guess that ain't the answer either."

The two men laugh.

Some say the day of the open range sheep herd is coming to an end. Inflation, and fuel and labor costs have kept the Parises from making a profit in recent years. But Beltran's grandson has bet all he has to buy a ranch of his own.

"I always admired the way grandpa done it," says Little Pete. "I'd just kinda like to try it myself to see if I could make a ranch work. You gotta take a chance."

Beltran Paris has taught his grandson something.

"There's worse things," he says, "than going bankrupt in pursuit of the American dream."

The Kind of Family
America Used to Know

Recently I met a man who bemoaned the fact that we were all
adrift in a sea of circumstance with no control over what we
might bump into. He had lost sight of the America he had known
as a child, the safe harbor of a strong family and secure work.
It bothered him that people are no longer known for what they
do, but for what they own.

Well, not much I said at the time could cheer him, but then,
I hadn't been to Great Bend, Kansas. Out there, under a cotton-
puff sky, I met the kind of family America used to hear about.
Wading across the wheat fields came Roger and David and their
nephew, Jay. Their dads work on the oil rigs. So do four older
brothers—ten hours a day, seven days a week.

They live in a house their parents bought two decades ago
for $140. A home their folks rebuilt in the quiet of their eve-
nings. Ten airtight rooms cooled and humidified by an indoor
pond. Heated and ventilated by wood-burning stoves.

"Winter before last, we still had our old floor furnace," said Reba Roach, the matriarch of the clan, "and our propane bill was twelve hundred dollars."

"What is it now?" I asked.

"Oh, let's see. What did we spend last year? I think about three hundred dollars."

The younger boys raise ducks and geese to pay for family vacations. Reba cans five hundred quarts of food from a backyard vegetable patch. Roger, not yet out of high school, dreams of joining his dad and big brothers on the oil rigs. They gave him some advice.

"If a person's going to give you a job," said Roger, "and you have a reputation of not being very good, your chances of getting that job will be real bad. But if you always do good work, no matter what, your chances of getting that job will be a lot better."

The Roaches' backyard is what Noah's ark might have looked like, had no one ever closed the door. The lame and the injured find their way here.

"Well, there's always room for little critters, I think," said Reba, wiping the feathers of a waterlogged chick. "I like kids and animals, I guess. I've sure had my share of both."

Reba has never needed an automatic dishwasher. She has raised seven children. The only gadget in her kitchen is an electric coffeepot, purchased when the boys started leaving home earlier and traveling farther to find work. They drive two hundred miles, round trip, every day. Hundreds of oil rigs closer to home have shut down.

It is a troubling time. High utility bills took the gas water heater. The family boils its water on the stove. Tough, but better than when they first moved in, with lots of diapers, and no running water.

"I needed water," said Reba. "I needed to wash for them, so I went and got snow. We melted it on the stove. It worked great! Softest water in town."

The family does not eat out often. It costs them sixty dollars for pizza. The married boys bring their kids next door to mamma's.

"I was born a hundred years too late," said Reba, watching the steam from her teapot cloud the windowpane. "If I had my way about it—oh, I can really get into this—if I had my way about it, we'd be totally, completely self-sufficient."

Reba's children cherish their independence, but they are worried. The wheat field around their house has a crop of FOR SALE signs. Despite their hard work, despite their frugality, their future is uncertain.

"Oh, we've got some set away," said Ken Roach. "We'll do okay, provided we don't live too long."

Dinner was over. The family spilled out onto the front lawn. Ducks scurried toward the pond. The kids went to work on a new fence. Reba covered a nesting bird with cardboard. The night looked like rain.

A Special Friendship

Ethan Allen Sapp lives alone in his grandfather's old house, a wooden plantation home that has been locked and dried by the sun and has turned the color of ash. It nestles partially hidden at the end of a moss-covered lane in New River, Florida.

Willie Mae Lightburn is alone, too, in a busy federal housing project in Pahokee, Florida. They are a lifetime away from each other, but their memories still cling.

"Them days is gone," says Willie Mae, shelling peas on her front porch. "They won't be no more."

"Daddy furnished the land and the mules and the plows," says Ethan Allen, "and he give Willie Mae's family half. Whatever they made, he gave them half."

Willie Mae and Ethan Allen are the last who can tell the story. One hundred and fifty years ago, his grandaddy bought her grandfather at an auction.

It was the start of a friendship.

"I think they did love each other," says Ethan Allen, "or they wouldn't have respected each other or cared for each other and tried to help each other as they did."

"We eat together, we play together," says Willie Mae. "Didn't cut no ice about the color."

There is nothing sentimental about slavery, but this is a story unique in our history. Something special happened between two families—one black, one white—that set them together against the grain of the times.

For nearly a century, their people bent over side by side in the field. And when slavery ended, they tried something their neighbors in New River never quite understood. They tried to live as equals.

The women helped each other give birth. The children shared their games. The men buried each family's dead in the old cemetery behind the farm house.

"What was it that your two families had between them?" I ask Ethan Allen, as we wander through the cemetery looking at headstones pitted with age.

"Well," he says, flicking a cricket from his cane, "I guess brotherly love would cover it. Wouldn't it?"

There was a muffled crack and drum of distant thunder. An almost invisible curtain of rain seemed to draw near as I ask Willie Mae, "Did you both share a dream?"

"We had to share it. If we hadn't shared, it never would have happened."

For three generations, their people were born and raised in the same old kitchen. They grew up together. Then, one by one, they began to leave.

They took with them their legacy of love. Willie Mae raised three families, including a white girl nobody wanted.

"Her mother died one week and her daddy died the next," she said. "That was pitiful. None of her people wanted her. And I told her, I said, 'Baby,' I said, 'you don't have to go over there.

Just stay right here.' I said, 'Christmas is coming, and I'm going to buy you some toys.' And I did."

Long after the two families had left the plantation, they kept in touch through announcements of births and deaths and holiday visits.

Willie Mae is ailing now. Ethan Allen has had a stroke. He still comes three hundred miles to see her.

"Who is this lady sitting here?" he says, shuffling up the side-walk. "Anybody know her?"

The neighbors stare as the aging white man takes off his cap and sits.

"You wanna hug my neck, Willie?" he says.

"Yeah, I wanna hug your neck."

"I tell you," she says, tugging at Ethan, "if I wasn't sick and

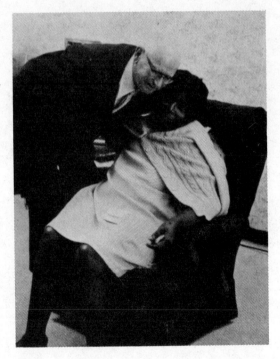

A hug for an old friend

down like I am, I would go back. I would go and stay with you. I would go and live with you."

Some friendships cannot be measured. They are the sum of a lifetime of kindness.

Homecoming

A friend of mine played football for a school so small that the players changed uniforms at half time and came back as the band. There were so few girls that they borrowed cheerleaders from another town. It made for some close relationships. My pal married a cheerleader. She also played the flute in the band. She also moved the yard markers. That's the way it is with small-town football—a family affair.

Is football important in west Texas? Does Mean Joe Greene like Cokes? On game days in Gordon, some people back their pickups to the field seven hours before kick off, while over at the Gordon drugstore, the coffee-cup coaches are still talking about last week's game.

"Those boys should'a remembered that other team is just like anybody else," says one man, tapping his cigarette on the Formica counter. "Those other ole boys put their pant legs on one leg at a time."

Football is more than just a game in Gordon—it is the rhythm of life. As sure as autumn follows summer, little girls grow up to be cheerleaders and little boys dream of Friday nights.

On this Friday evening, Lloyd Whitlock leads the pep parade. He has a special talent. Whitlock can so faithfully imitate a fire engine's siren that dalmatians have been known to track him for days.

Pickups carrying most of the town follow behind. That causes something of a problem: finding someone to wave to. For as long as anyone can remember, Gordon has closed its doors in the golden sun of autumn to follow its team. If you want a cigar or a corn plaster, you've got to get it before Lloyd Whitlock sings his siren song.

There are so many tiny Texas towns like Gordon that they have formed their own football league, fielding six-man teams. In six-man football, there are only three men on the line, and anyone can go out for a pass. It makes for some wide-open games. If either side gets forty-five points ahead, they call it quits and go to the American Legion hall for fun.

There is more here than cheerleaders and players looking for careers. I hesitate to use the word "cozy," for it seems so out of place in football. But the field in Gordon, Texas, is, well, "cozy." Take Carrie Teichner, for example. She comes to hear the band. She's part of the family, and she is blind.

On this night, the thumping of a big bass drum sends Carrie into an ecstasy of giggles. You can just feel the excitement. Gordon may not have invented the word "homecoming," but it has given it special meaning.

Catfish Caller

In the age-old battle between man and fish, man has mounted quite an armada. Weekend anglers zip across lakes with military precision, tracking fish in high-speed boats with sonar and automatic pilot, fancy rods and reels, and lures that sing like crickets in the night.

Herman Coussens never joined that armada. Whenever he wants fish, he just floats out on his farm pond and calls them for dinner—theirs and his.

What happens next is not to be believed. Hundreds of catfish race across Herman's five-acre lake to get a little meal of cottonseed and bread.

"They like a voice that's tender and loving," says Coussens, "just like a woman. I tell women, 'My name is Coussens, Kissin' Coussens,' and they usually throw a cheek over and let me kiss 'em. That's the way these catfish are. They know I'm not going to hurt 'em." He grins. "Oh, once in a while I'll catch one."

Some folks don't think fish come to Herman just because he calls. Scientists believe he has them conditioned to respond. Kind of like Pavlov's dogs, who were trained to eat every time a light flashed. Well, Pavlov's dogs didn't come from five acres away.

The fellows down at the Talihina Lions Club kid Herman about his talent, but they've all enjoyed the fifteen thousand catfish he has pulled from his pond.

"Hey, Herman," laughs one man as he slices into his meal, "I was wondering if this was one of your pets."

"Naw," smiles Herman. "Just a cousin."

When Herman's nine grandchildren drop by with some of the neighborhood kids, all they need are a few cane poles, a cricket or two and a quick arm.

"When you hook a mess of fish," says Coussens to his tiny granddaughter, "they quit bitin'. Grandma taught them to do that way."

Within ten minutes the four-year-old and her brothers and sisters have reeled in twenty-two fish. Herman dumps them in a sack and heads up the hill.

"Let's see if Grandma will cook these up for us," says Coussens. "Come on, you kids. Drop your poles and help us carry or we can't get all this to the kitchen."

What's Herman's secret? He's been feeding these fish for fifteen years. Most of the time, he leaves them alone.

Now, before you come looking for this pied piper and his magic pond, remember, "Only children and veterans are allowed to fish here," calls Herman over his shoulder.

World War I veterans. *Wounded* World War I veterans.

"Facing the Morning Sun"

I was reading a quote this morning from a fellow who is little known for his philosophy.

He wrote: "Sometimes when a man climbs the ladder of success, he finds that it's been leaning against the wrong wall."

The philosopher's name was Richard Nixon.

Did you ever stop to wonder what your life would have been like had you followed your first dream? A. W. Yeats wondered, and at age seventy-two, he decided to do just that.

I found him near the ceiling of an old cathedral, ducking between the gray pipes and the sunbeams, restoring a church organ. He was working each piece by hand, something he has done without salary for half a dozen churches in south Texas. What drives a man at seventy-two to work high up where the bats fly?

"My daddy fell out of a pecan tree when he was ninety," says Yeats, "and I'm his son."

Well, there is more, much more. For most of his life, A. W. Yeats never put a bolt to a nut. He was an English professor who surrounded himself with books. Rare books of great beauty and surprise.

"Books must be special," says Yeats, pulling an old leather-bound volume from the shelf in his study, "and in order to make a book extra special, the French had a device. Instead of just putting pictures on pages, they put a lovely water color on the outside edge. It only appears when all the pages are bunched together."

He paused. With the book closed, the edges of the pages became a study of pastels and Renaissance gold.

"In every work of genius," he continues, "we see our own rejected thoughts." Yeats laughs long and low. "I've been as much a mystery to myself as anything. I'm not right sure I've got all my eggs in one basket yet.

"You're looking at a man who's grasping for a place in society. It's no fun not to have any children, not to have a wife. You have to tie yourself to the people with whom you live. If you don't, you're adrift."

Yeats replaces the book.

"I saw the time once when I wanted to commit suicide." He stares at the shelf without seeing. "There was that much grief and that much anguish."

What changed his mind?

"Facing the morning sun," says Yeats. "I told myself, 'Get off your fanny and get your courage back in your gizzard and go to work.'"

The professor added to his neighborhood of words. He built a new home next to folks who worked with their hands for a living and touched the talents he had learned as a boy. Most teachers write books when they retire . . . A. W. Yeats chose to do his writing in iron and wood.

"It's more permanent," he says. "Ninety-seven percent of all the books printed between 1900 and 1950 will be pulp and dust by the end of this century. And I figure that if you make a fine clock, fine woodwork, it stays longer."

In his workshop, A. W. Yeats sets his own pace, his own standards, and if some hours are less astonishing than he had hoped, they are, for better or worse, in his own hands.

Country Mardi Gras

MAMOU, LOUISIANA
(1981)

To some, the Mardi Gras means fancy masked balls and big parades, or thousands spent on costumes and parties. But for a Cajun in Mamou, the celebration costs only seven dollars and fifty cents. For that, he gets beer, hard boiled eggs, sausage, and the answer to the age-old question, "Why did the chicken cross the road?"

In Mamou, it's to keep a step ahead of the stewpot.

"Give that chicken an even chance to run!" yelled a cowboy wearing a goblin's mask.

The fleeing fowl flew across the field. Fifty horsemen dressed in Mardi Gras costumes thundered in pursuit. The frightened hen was more agile than its pursuers. And it had one other advantage.

"The chicken is sober," laughed one horseman, "and most of us ain't."

Mardi Gras in Mamou

It is a country tradition in Mamou for Mardi Gras revelers to charge into farmyards and beg for chickens. If the farmer agrees, they chase his gift like a feathered football, hoping to pop it into a pot of gumbo. Great care is taken to keep the competition even. Horsemen are searched for weapons before they join the chase. Chickens are given time to talk to Thanksgiving turkeys who've survived.

Mamou is one of the last towns to carry on this tradition of "country" Mardi Gras untouched by tourists or commercialism. It is more than a social event. It is a rite of passage. Young men must wait until their sixteenth birthdays to take their places beside the adults.

The joy and the music meander along the back roads of the parish. Seven hours of beer and bouncing and chickens that dare to think they're in charge.

After a while, most of the riders are no longer horsemen.

"We still got five hours to go?" one man blinked incredulously.

"How you holdin' up?" asked his partner.

"Oh, I don't know," said the first man. "This Zorro is about to give it up."

Moments later, he was added to a pile of drunken revelers stacked on a flatbed truck that rambled behind the procession.

Mardi Gras in Mamou is a celebration that ranks next to weddings and funerals for bringing families back home.

"When you're born and raised in Mamou," said a man, trotting up to the beer truck, "and you drink the Mamou water, you always come back."

For the boy passing into manhood, there is a great truth beneath the flutter of feathers: life has its winners and losers, on both sides.

"Hey, throw me a chicken," said a kid, from the back of a flatbed wagon. "I haven't gotten one all day."

"Go tell it to Colonel Sanders!" cried someone in the crowd.

The Bargain

Back when Zachary Taylor was running for president, the letter announcing his nomination arrived without a stamp. Now, most politicians would pay their last penny to receive such a note, but not old Zachary. For one month, he refused to pay the ten-cents postage due. Fortunately, he had a persistent postman, or he might never have been president.

Folks in Magnolia Springs, Alabama, have such a letter carrier. Jamie James takes the mailman's motto to heart. Out here, the rain and the snow and the gloom of night are not nearly as troublesome as the wind and the fog—and the hurricanes.

Jamie James is the only postman in the country who still delivers the mail, house to house, by boat.

Six days a week, Jamie churns the remote coastal creeks of southern Alabama. He makes his twenty-five-mile run in an open boat no bigger than a bathtub. Low-hanging branches near shore keep him from using a more comfortable conveyance. Waves along the coastline sometime reach six feet. Noah's ark could have set sail on the morning we caught up with him.

"The first sixty days after I took this job," said Jamie, "I was wet forty-seven straight trips. I thought I was a duck."

Duck, maybe. Fish, no.

"I can't swim," said Jamie, racing under a wave that seemed as big as Baltimore. "I was in the navy twenty-seven years and they never did teach me to swim. Would you mind handing me that bailing bucket?"

Why does he do this?

"I like it!"

Clearly Jamie James goes to work for more than a pay check. Out in his boat, alone against the wind, he is moved by the same spirit that put men into planes to sail over barns. Skimming the shore, stirring reflections of pine and cypress, Jamie is a mirror of another time.

His neighbors, the 175 families who live along this remote route, have come to depend on Jamie. He comes when others do not.

"Hey, Jamie! I'm over here!" cried a woman in a housecoat. "The rain has flooded the box. It floated off somewhere."

"Hang on," called Jamie. "I'll paddle over to you."

The woman waded out where her wharf should have been. Jamie nudged his small boat against the current.

"I don't mind fast water," said Jamie, flashing a crinkled smile in the rain. "Keeps the alligators down. Just to be safe, though, I wouldn't splash my hand over the side. They're liable to think you're groceries."

"Want to tie up for some coffee?" yelled the woman.

"Nah, thanks," said Jimmy, holding his oar for her to grab. "Gotta check on the others."

Such neighborly attention is remarkable in this age of faceless bureaucracy. Jamie brings letters and mails packages. But he also carries the news. He is his neighbors' daily link to each other. Is it surprising, then, that at one time the Postal Service was not sure Jamie was worth it? Several years ago, it wanted to eliminate the water route, until Jamie's neighbors pointed out that the taxpayer got Jamie, his boat, and the gas to run it for eight thousand dollars a year.

Oh, and something more—they got a friend.

That's a bargain . . . even in Zachary Taylor's book.

Swamp Fire

The ancient, awesome Okefenokee Swamp is one of the most primitive areas on earth, a swamp so big you could lose New York City. It is not voices that reach over this swamp but echoes, sounds of misty dawns and silken days, stretching undisturbed for six thousand years.

The Okefenokee is a strange carpet of floating islands, vast prairies that shift to the touch like water beds. Left to itself, the Okefenokee would fill with vegetation and become a forest. Rooting trees and bushes would stabilize the islands. But the swamp has survived because of fire.

Every twenty years or so, in times of drought, a great purging blaze burns out the vegetation and reverses this natural process. The last one, in 1954, burned for more than a year. Ralph Davis called it the Mule Tail fire, a fearsome thing that switched out of the swamp and swept over his farm and forest.

"Why, it even sucked all the ashes off the ground," said

Davis. "Wasn't any ashes left. It was just like you swept them with a broom."

All that seems natural to a man who has spent his seventy years living next to the Okefenokee. Davis has mapped and hunted almost every inch and is now a guide.

"Folks around here," I laughed, stepping into his swamp boat, "say that they gave you a job with the federal government to keep you from poaching."

"Well, some truth in that," chuckled Davis. "Yeah, some truth."

"How many alligators did you get in one night?" I asked.

"Thirty-eight," said Davis. "Thirty-eight is all you'd want in the boat at one time."

We pushed off into the canal. The dock disappeared behind us as we slid into a tangle of green vines. Huge black lumps—alligators—circled the boat.

The alligators were a sure sign of new drought. The water was so low, that our boat bumped along their backs. Most of

Ralph Davis pushes off into the swamp

the swamp trails were now too shallow for travel. In places, the Okefenokee looked like Kansas.

Ironically, the concern is not that the swamp may be too dry and ready to burn, but that it may still be too wet for the vast purging fire it needs to survive. After the Mule Tail blaze, the government built a dam to keep the Okefenokee from drying up. The cycle of big fires was too costly.

Great stands of pine surround the swamp. They are cultivated forests that produce turpentine, timber, and pulp wood. The dam protects that property, but may also alter the balance in the swamp. Researchers have begun to study the effect the barrier is having.

"We soon won't have no prairies in this swamp," said Davis. "You'll have a few trails if they keep them opened up with trail cutters, and you'll have canals in some of your main places, but that will be it."

Can the Okefenokee survive? The sound of the swamp—the croaking and cawing of a huge discordant symphony—overwhelms a man's thoughts on that question. But it reminds us that in the end, nature does not play by man's rules.

"A Man Ain't Nothing
But a Man"

They say if you listen quietly up here on Big Bend Mountain, you can still hear hammering, Old John Henry's ghost fighting progress with his big, broad arm. Legend has it that John Henry fought his famous battle with the steam drill near here, man against machine to see who could lay more railroad track. John Henry won, but then he collapsed, dead of a broken heart. His legend still clings to the valley like the mist, and its drama has inspired a unique theater.

Each spring, neighbors near Talcott, West Virginia, take time to listen to the tales their old-timers have to tell, tales of John Henry and the place where he died.

"There's something strange about that tunnel," says an old man, pointing to the mountain where John Henry fought the steam drill. "Around dusk, the fog comes out of that hole and swirls around you, and it feels warm, not cold."

John Henry's legend has passed in song throughout the world, but the memory of his life lives only in this valley. Each summer, neighbors gather to pass on what they know and to produce a play based on what they have learned from each other.

It is no mere pageant. It is theater that comes from the home. Maryat Lee opens her barn on Powleys Creek for practice. James Dodd's agriculture class builds the stage on the back of a hay wagon.

The kids feel comfortable with one another and know their subject well. The theater has become a part of the valley.

"We're not actors from a million miles away," says Mike Buckland, waiting backstage in a cornfield. "The people know us, and we know them. That's why this theater works."

The show is not slick. It doesn't have much of a budget. Patrons sit on lawn chairs. Blankets and ice coolers stretch far up the hill.

"A machine three times as fast as me!"

The young girl's voice struggles to lift past the moths that flutter in the spotlight.

"I ain't sure about that, Captain."

No one seems to notice that John Henry is being played by a girl.

"A man ain't nothing but a man. But before I let that steam drill beat me, I'll die with my hammer in my hands!"

A tiny girl in the audience turns her face to her mother in wonder. The mother pulls her close. On stage, the contest between the steam drill and John Henry begins.

The audience claps. The sledge hammers tap. The performance rings out across the valley.

The theater is just a small pinpoint of light that shatters at play's end and seems to explode as headlights search for home.

Folks will return next year. The play is changed every time another memory is added. People come again and again to see what new stories have been found and to see themselves reflected.

The grit, the endurance of John Henry's life touches something special. Somewhere up on Big Bend Mountain, Ol' John Henry is tap hammering his applause.

FIVE

A Need for Beauty

"...*shake hands with Big Mamma Nature*"
CARROLL ABBOTT

Poem Without a Pen

FRANCONIA, NEW HAMPSHIRE
(1984)

In 1915, poet Robert Frost brought his wife and four children to a small farm in the White Mountains of New Hampshire. He was a terrible farmer. He used to milk the cows at midnight so he could sleep late. His neighbors in nearby Franconia, New Hampshire, figured he'd be on the town's welfare rolls by Christmas.

A lot of town folks wondered what Ol' Bob was doing when he lived out there. He wasn't real famous yet. People saw him swinging on trees or stopping in their woods. Even his little horse thought he was strange. He never could decide which road to take.

One day, they heard Robert Frost read something he had written.

"The woods are lovely, dark, and deep,
But I have promises to keep,

And miles to go before I sleep,
And miles to go before I sleep."

Here, in Franconia, Robert Frost would become America's best-known poet.

Much has changed since then, but the people of Franconia never forgot Robert Frost. His old homestead came up for sale a few years back, and the town, all 760 of the people who live there, bought it. Taxed themselves a bundle to get it.

"Every man, woman, and child. Probably some of the dogs. Twenty-five bucks a person," says David Schaffer, the town's moderator.

People figured if the place worked for Frost, it could work for others. Each year for eight years, they have paid poets to live in the home.

"We wanted it to go on serving poetry," said Van Machlin, a retired college professor and co-founder of the project. "Not just to sit there as a dusty museum, but to be alive with living people in it, writing poetry."

It is no museum.

Ben Santos learned to walk here, flipping over the antique footstool in Frost's front room. Ben's father, Rod Santos, is the poet this year. Rod is thirty-four, a former University of Missouri professor who won the 1982 National Poetry Award. The town picks writers who are still young but already recognized —as near to the stage in their careers as Frost was at the time he lived there. They get the house—rent free—with a salary. And only an occasional visitor.

"Once someone came through the house," said Santos, a slight smile on his face. "He walked outside and was standing on the front porch, and he said, 'That Jack Frost could sure write some good poems, couldn't he?'"

The view from Robert Frost's front porch is poetic, of course. The White Mountains ripple away in the distance. But Rod and his wife, Lynne Manne, also a published poet, spend their days inside with the curtains drawn. Poetry is seldom written

The Frost house in Franconia

looking out. Writing is memory, not moment. Words must be filtered through emotion. Robert Frost once said, "A poem begins with a lump in the throat."

What effect has living in Robert Frost's place had on their poetry? Lynne Manne said: "To look at things the way they [the Frosts] looked at them frees you in a strange sort of way. Because then you can begin to see where you're different. I'm more interested in the domestic landscape. What it means to be a mother. What it means to be a wife. When we sit in that kitchen drinking our coffee, we can see Eleanor at the stove telling Robert to get to work, goading him to write another poem. And I think, maybe that presence is still there doing that to us."

The sun is setting, warm and red. The woods behind the house lose their color. Ben has had his bath in Frost's old tub.

Rod sits reading at an upstairs window. Lynne tucks the baby in.

"One little poem before you go night-night. Okay? This one's about you.

> "All the little ones I never had,
> Keep vigil with me,
> drawstrings tucked.
> Now they want their starlight,
> Their glasses of milk,
> Their story."

Franconia could have built a basketball court or a new bridge with its tax money. It did not.

It wrote a poem—without a pen.

Mr. Flowers

There isn't a politician in America who wasn't elected on the promise to fight professional interests. You know the campaign slogan, "Now you have a friend in the capital." Well, a lot of other people do, too. In Texas alone, there are 753 professional lobbyists working for nearly one thousand different causes.

One man on the list says his major concern is himself. Another wants to "revive the armadillos." The president of Marijuana Enterprises didn't give his address. And then there's Carroll Abbott, the only registered lobbyist in the state of Texas —for wild flowers.

I found him on a grassy rise covered in purple and gold, flecked with red and black, a blanket of wild flowers in first bloom. He climbs into view from behind a small hill, moving easily, like a man who cares little for neckties. A battered hat shadows his sun-wrinkled face. His cowboy boots shift lightly, side to side, as he carefully steps between the clumps of wild flowers. He stops to light a cigarette, then brings a magnifying glass to his eye and squints through a haze of smoke at a small flower.

"I kept trying to get the other guy to do it," says Abbott, "and one day I said to myself, 'Hey, man, if you really believe that this is worth doing, then why don't you do it!' "

Abbott wanted a Texas wild flower day and started a company to sell the idea.

"Sank plum out of sight the first three years," he admits. "Boy, was it tough. I mean, we didn't hit rock bottom; we went all the way through that thing."

But Abbott gathers strength from his constituents, the beautiful wild flowers of the Texas hill country.

"We lived on hopes and dreams for years and years and years," he says, "but I didn't get discouraged. You cannot have bluebonnets except in spring." He paused to watch a caravan of cars stop along the highway below. Tourists take turns taking pictures of one another in the field of wild flowers. "Each thing has a fullness of its own season," Abbott continues. "You can't hurry it, so we just kept working."

When his bill finally got to the floor of the Texas legislature, it passed the house in twenty-six seconds. "Stalled in the senate for two and a half minutes," Abbott recalls. William Clements, who was governor then, took one minute to sign.

The lobbyist laughs, "Who could be against wild flowers?"

Abbott spent half his life as a newspaperman before becoming a saver of plants. There are more than five thousand kinds of wild flowers in Texas, nearly one-fourth of all the varieties that grow in the United States. They look fragile, but they are tough, unwrinkled by sandpaper winds.

People crowding the prairie, building great cities and suburbs, do what the winds cannot. Pastures become skylines. Houses blossom on hills. Yet the wild flowers still cling.

"They were here a long, long time before we were," says Abbott, touching a petal, "and I have the suspicion they're going to be here a long time after we're gone."

His family lived on borrowed money while he taught himself the secret of the Texas wild flowers, a secret he relates to visitors with a slight grin and a dry laugh: "A weed is only a plant in a place you don't want it."

Abbott's wife, Pat, sells the tiny seeds he harvests on his walks.

"You don't sneeze when you're working with these," says Pat, rolling a sack for a mail-order client. "You could blow your whole profit for a week."

The morning sun shimmers blue against her window. She can see her husband on the hillside beyond the highway. A slight wind shakes the dew. Small petals open to the warmth of the day. Carroll Abbott has been up for some time as if he sensed that the season would not wait for sleepyheads. He pauses to put another bud into a tricorner slip of paper, examining it first through his magnifying glass.

"Isn't that beautiful!" he mumbles, twisting the glass before his eye. He shakes his head, and smiles and looks up. "There are a great many things in this world that aren't equivalent to money or fine fashion or good food." Abbott wraps the seeds and tucks them in his pocket. "You know," he says, scanning the flowers that rippled away to the horizon, "there's a peace and serenity that comes when you get out and shake hands with big Mamma Nature."

The lobbyist shuffles slowly down the hill. Once again, his eyes are firmly fixed on the ground. Carroll Abbott is making his rounds in the halls of true power, a world wrapped in cobweb paper, awash with bees and butterflies and ants—an endless kaleidoscope of color.

"Footprints"

It is a world of fire and ice: a teakettle land of boiling steam and belly-deep snow. Sands as hot as a sauna. Air as cold as sixty below. Only the strong and the stubborn survive.

A fellow by the name of John Colter was the first man to tell the world about Yellowstone. He was a mountain man who had come West with Lewis and Clark and stayed on to hunt and trap. One day, after seven years and a particuarly close call with a band of Indians who wanted to make him bald before his time, Colter announced that he would leave the great Yellowstone land forever. He jumped into a canoe and paddled all the way to St. Louis without stopping—two thousand miles in one month.

Nobody back east believed his fancy tales of hot springs and boiling mud. People thought there might be a crystal heaven somewhere out West, but if there were a hell, they said, it was Colter's hell.

Well, even today, few people have seen this great yellowstone land in winter when hell freezes over.

The waters that flow through Yellowstone are rivers of life. Heated by runoff and steam, they melt the snow and provide a foggy grocery store for the animals that huddle close.

Into this silent world comes a figure—somehow oddly out of place—moving carefully through the massive, dark shapes.

Alone.

For twenty years, Wolfgang Bayer has traveled the world for Walt Disney and for the *National Geographic*, showing us a side of nature we seldom see.

"It still fascinates me," says Bayer. "There's still a lot that I can discover. That I can portray on film."

Wolfgang Bayer lives just outside the park. Each winter, he hikes its two million acres, recording life in the snow.

One of Yellowstone's winter residents

"I'm at home here," says the photographer, using his camera tripod as a ski pole. Patience is his most important tool. He has been known to wait two weeks for just the right shot.

"One morning there I was," says Wolfgang, "minding my own business filming coyotes. I thought I was in a pretty good position, hiding behind a tree, bending over the camera as I usually do, when all of a sudden, I felt this very sharp pain in my butt. I turned around. A coyote actually snuck up, bit me, and took off again.

"The human race tends to think they're so sophisticated and smart but, in reality, the animals have to be smarter. They have less to go by in order to survive."

Ten feet away, a buffalo stands knee-deep in water, eating aquatic plants. His head is the size of a redwood stump. (Bison are the largest land animals in the New World.) This fellow probably weighs more than a ton. He takes a step. Icicles hanging from his fur coat chime, crack, and cascade into the river. He looks up. His eyes are soft and brown and merely curious. The steam rising off the water shifts with the wind. The buffalo disappears.

Wolfgang Bayer steps back from his viewfinder.

"Have you had any close calls?" I ask.

"Oh, yeah, quite a few. I've been chased up trees by rhinos and elephants. Been mauled by a jaguar. That happened in the bathroom of all things."

"In a bathroom?"

"Yeah, yeah. We had a tame jaguar in California when we did a film down there. And someone put him in the bathroom. I was in there too. I wound up behind the jaguar. The jaguar is between me and the door. So I sat there and thought, then tried to step over the jaguar to get to the door. You just don't do this. You don't step over an animal that size. Every time I stepped over him, he bit me in the leg. I was speeding around, you know, kicking, and the jaguar was sort of growling. My wife was standing outside. She thought it was the last of me."

Bayer chuckles.

"She called the insurance company."

"How did you get out?" I ask

"The jaguar got tired."

Not all wildlife photography is done in the wild. Bayer's wife and children help him build elaborate sets for close-up work at home. They live on a hillside in Jackson, Wyoming. The close-up studio is in their basement.

That evening they were trying to film a rabbit.

"Okay, I'm rolling," says Wolfgang, ducking out from behind his camera. His six-year-old son, Tristan, lowers the rabbit into a man-made tunnel. His wife, Candice, adjusts the lights. Three-year-old Kristina sticks her head into the other end of the tunnel and coaxes the critter along.

"Is he coming?" asks Wolfgang.

The rabbit sniffs the shadow's edge beyond his man-made hole.

"And . . . *action!*" he cries.

"He isn't coming," says his wife.

The rabbit turns deeper into the darkness. He thinks he's a turtle.

Patience is not a tool just for the woods.

Wolfgang Bayer was born in Austria forty-six years ago. He came to this country to work for Chrysler but was laid off and headed West. On his own, he shot his first film, a half-hour movie that cost him two thousand dollars and sold for two hundred and fifty. It's subject was Yellowstone National Park.

"It took me fifteen years to find out that some of the best qualities in nature are right in front of my door," says Wolfgang the next morning. We were up at first light, walking among the bubbling caldrons and geysers.

Two million people watch Old Faithful erupt in summer. In winter, it shares the dawn with an elk.

"His only concern," says Wolfgang, setting up his tripod,

is survival, feeding. He couldn't care less what's behind him, the scenic splendor. Old Faithful going off is nothing to him."

The huge geyser rumbles and explodes, cracking its icy cover and draping the trees with crystalized steam. The surrounding forest looks like an army of ghosts.

Wolfgang slides behind his eyepiece to record a world the tourist seldom sees. His telephoto lens focuses on small bugs called brine flies, which live just an inch above the boiling water. They dive into the whirling froth, protected by a bubble of air to feed on the algae. If they go too low, they boil—too high, they freeze. They live out their lives in an inch of space.

There are about one million different kinds of animals in the world. Wolfgang Bayer has filmed two hundred. Today he will stalk through the snow in temperatures thirty below, wait for

Waiting for the perfect shot

eight hours, and perhaps find one more. I asked him if he ever tired of this great task.

"I just take pictures," he said, strapping on his snowshoes and crunching away toward the next geyser. "They are everything I love. I leave nothing but footprints."

"My Mind's Eye"

NORTHERN NEW MEXICO
(1979)

The Sangre de Cristo Mountains have been an inspiration for generations of artists. Each morning as the sun slips over the horizon, the paint pot tips and spills, casting its beauty on the people below. Life in the valley flows in rhythm with that beauty. Sculptors work the morning light, move with the morning sun.

Michael Naranjo has lived in these mountains all his life. He is an artist, but for him the sun's beauty is only memory.

Michael Naranjo is blind.

Naranjo lost his sight in Vietnam. Took up sculpturing to find new visions. Now he is creating a ten-foot, four-thousand-pound statue—all by touch.

"I was sitting in my living room one day," says Naranjo, "and saw this gray shadow moving across in front of me. It was my mind's eye that was looking at it. And, suddenly, the shadow formed. It was an eagle dancer. When I looked close

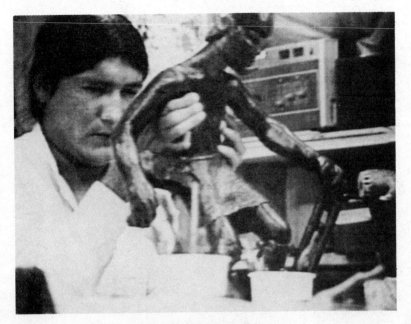

Michael Naranjo at work

it disappeared. But I had seen it, so I could bring it back to my mind's eye."

The sculpture he saw was a vivid shadow of his Indian heritage. Naranjo grew up in one of the pueblos that line the valley. His life on the reservation left an enormous wealth of memory. In the eleven years since that first vision, he has cast forty bronze sculptures.

"They are my children," says Naranjo. "I struggled with them in thought and in their creation. And, suddenly, they were very strong within, and they had to come out."

Michael's loss has intensified his appreciation of life. In the tenth year of his blindness, he married. His wife, Laurie, is his model and his eyes.

"I'm happy. I'm very happy," says Michael. "My life is full because of sculpture. If I had a choice of sight or sculpture, I wouldn't take sight."

Nature's Painter

FLOWERY BRANCH, GEORGIA
(1981)

American folk art is flowering. Galleries from New York to Los Angeles report a blooming interest. Collectors move through the countryside as aggressively as antique dealers. Almost every town has a museum these days. An old railroad caboose houses the art in Flowery Branch, Georgia. Well, some of the art. Not all.

Listen for the locomotive's call. Follow it along the tracks to the field beyond the museum to the place where Carlton Garrett has spent his life.

Carlton Garrett is a working man, not one for museums. But on cold, clear weekends and on a thousand lunch hours, he has retreated into a world of his own—a world he whittles out of wood.

In the fragrant closeness of his toolshed, Carlton Garrett has traced his life in toys. Each toy is an elaborate polished memory from his past. Not just life as he lived it, but life as he would have liked it to be, perfected by a wood-carver's hand.

"I never made no diagram or nothin'," says Garrett. "I just got it in my head, and at bedtime after I went to bed, it would just come to my mind, and I'd know what to do."

Garrett first made toys to entertain his kids, but long after the children had grown and gone, he continued whittling for himself.

"No, I'm not an artist," he says, thumbing a sliver of wood. "I'm just an old jackleg—a little bit of everything."

Most of his life, Carlton Garrett worked with machines, building what the world told him to build. He has great love and respect for technology, but his favorite toy shows man's first fight with progress: a carving of John Henry, the steel-driving man. He had whittled it into hundreds of interconnected parts, powered by a small motor. When plugged in, John Henry's tiny figure does eternal battle with the machine.

"Which is more important to you, the man or the machine?" I ask.

Garrett pauses a long, long time before answering, "The man."

Carlton Garrett's life stands as a reminder that in each of us there is some creative potential, perhaps not for art galleries or big museums, but a tool shed is not a bad place, either.

"I'm proud somebody thinks I am an artist," says Garrett, pulling another stool up to his bench. "Sit down and stay awhile?"

There are two kinds of creative people: Folks who study and struggle to promote their work and please an audience and those who seek to satisfy only themselves. It's tougher to find the second kind. Their work seldom shows up in a caboose.

Remember that first picture you brought home from school? The one you drew with a Crayola as fat as a Lincoln log and stuck proudly on the ice box. So proud.

In Fayette, Alabama, I met a man who drew his first picture in the dirt. It washed away with the evening rains, but the thrill of that first effort kept him painting and posting his art wherever he found an empty space. He never had time for formal training, never went to town for art supplies. He made his own, from nature.

Jimmy Lee Suddath is seventy now, but like Peter Pan, he never grew up. Each morning, he still wanders the forest near his home, searching for a rainbow of colors.

He finds his red in the cat's paw bush; gets his green from the turnips that grow in the garden. The countryside is his canvas. He paints on what he collects—old doors, washing machine lids, broken shutters. On them all, he creates detailed portraits made of mud.

"I don't like to use a paintbrush," says Jimmy Lee, stirring water into a Pet Milk can filled with dirt. "I like to use something from where I started." He dips a twig into the goo. A

The colors of the earth

174

small glop clings to its tip. He trowels it onto a board. "See how quickly you can paint with mud? You can't do that with oils."

Jimmy Lee mixes what he finds in nature with twenty-two kinds of dirt to get the colors he needs. He likes to match his mud to the subject whenever possible.

"You know, I was in Washington," he says, "and got some earth from the White House." He leans back. "It weren't no account," he laughs. "That's right. Wouldn't stick to the board." Jimmy Lee cackles. "Like a lot of them big folks up there. Weren't no good. No, you can't paint with Washington dirt. It's the poorest dirt you ever did see."

What colors Jimmy Lee can't find in nature, he mixes around the house. Coffee grounds make a great brown. Flour makes fine snow. Exhaust from the lawn mower makes a passable black.

His secret ingredient comes from the grocery store. Sixty years ago, Jimmy Lee learned that his paintings wouldn't stick unless he mixed in something sweet, so he adds a dab of honey.

"That won't come off," he laughs. "The board will rot out under the picture. The paint will still be there."

Jimmy Lee is constantly looking for new colors. He watches an oil rig go up near his home; and while some men see money, Jimmy dreams of mud.

"They're playing in my paint box!" he cries over the noise of the drilling. "They're bringing up some paint for me."

What would his life have been like had he not found dirt?

"I don't know. I guess I'da been dead. You see, if you ain't doing nothing, you get lonesome, so I remember the things I see, and at night I can just see 'em, imagine how things look. I just sit there and imagine things and I paint them."

Why has he filled his life with paintings?

"I wanted something," says Jimmy Lee, "something that somebody else ain't got. I *got* something somebody else ain't got."

"Oh, See Me,
Charlotte Bergen"

The mirrors seldom see movement. The doors are mostly closed. But music comes from a solitary window, six hours a day, seven days a week. Inside, Charlotte Bergen lives her life, alone with the beauty she creates.

Charlotte Bergen was born to music and to money. She was a shy child who preferred the classics to her classmates. Her mother provided her with tutors, and her father told her simply, "live life deeply."

"Finish what you start," she says, resting her bow on the strings of her cello. "That is one of the things my dear parents used to say to me." She looks and sounds like Katharine Hepburn. "In the evening, when my father would come home, he'd walk up this little hallway here and his shoes, the type he wore then, would squeak, squeak. He'd look in on me and say, 'Still hard at it?' I'd say, 'Yes, Daddy, still hard at it'."

Other young women married and moved away, but Charlotte shut herself off, searching for the perfect note.

For forty-five years, Charlotte Bergen played the cello alone. Then something happened that changed her life. Her church asked her to conduct a music program. She took the challenge. At the age of sixty-nine, Charlotte Bergen went public, not just at the church but in a concert hall. And not just any concert hall:—Carnegie Hall.

All the feelings that she had bottled up for so long, broke loose.

Four times that first year, Charlotte Bergen paid forty thousand dollars to rent Carnegie Hall and the American Symphony Orchestra for her own concert season, fulfilling a dream she had had since seeing the great conductor, Toscanini.

"I remember sitting with my mother and father," she says, "and as I watched him conduct, I found myself becoming more and more intrigued with the conductor's stick. Finally, I leaned forward." She shifts closer. "And I said to myself, 'I wonder what it feels like to stand there and swing that little stick?'"

When she found out, concerts became the new passion of her life. For years thereafter, she continued to practice and pay for her own performances.

That afternoon, after Charlotte had finished her rehearsal, we sat in the vast parlor of her twenty-three-room mansion. A giant stuffed peacock stood at the foot of the main stairway behind us. A wooden ship she had built as a girl was to our side, and everywhere there were clutters of sheet music.

"You're a person who is terribly shy," I begin. "What did you have to tell yourself to get Charlotte Bergen to step out on that stage at Carnegie Hall?"

She smiles and strikes a determined pose.

"The very first time I walked out there," says Charlotte, bringing her hand to the side of her face, "I remember as I left the Green Room and approached the podium; saw it coming closer, closer, closer, I said to myself, 'Now see here, Bergen, you get out there. You step up there and you start swinging!'"

In her seventies, Charlotte Bergen broke her back when she tumbled from a ten-ton yellow tractor. She had been plowing her two-hundred-acre farm. The injury did not stop her. She still waits for her one visitor a day, the chauffeur, who brings a pint of ice cream at noon. It is the only break Charlotte Bergen allows herself during her concert season. She practices four hours a day, listening to records and waving her baton to an empty room.

"Music is constant," she says. "It is not like a sunset, which you can't control. It is feeling, not sound." A blending of the head, the heart, and the hand.

When she is ready, she gives tickets to anyone who will come see her.

"Some folks might say that what you're doing at Carnegie Hall is an extravagant way to spend your money."

Charlotte dismisses the remark with a wave of her baton.

"What do you think? I just go there to flourish around and say, 'Oh, see me, Charlotte Bergen. I'm going to rush out in a moment. I have a tea party I must attend!' "

She is insulted.

"To me, it would be highly immoral to bring a frivolous and surface attitude toward that great music."

Charlotte sniffs.

"I could help them build an orphanage here or there. Do any of a dozen things. I wouldn't know anything about it. I'd just dump money in other people's hands.

She shrugs and settles back in her chair.

"I'm a live part of this music. Now don't get me riled. I'm a *live part* of it, man! The gift without the giver is bare."

"What do you think about how you have lived your life?" I ask.

"I haven't finished living it yet. I'm only eighty-one!" she snaps.

She is indignant for a moment more; then her eyes twinkle.

"I'll tell you later on or get them to tell you."

Well, we don't have long to wait. The audience loves her,

and so do the critics. Her concerts fill quickly. Thousands have to be turned away. People come to enjoy, but they get something more.

"I think they carry away what I bring there," says Charlotte, "the love of it all. It's where words cease and music begins."

The Glass Harp

When the Renaissance Players perform in Miami, Jay Brown tunes up with a turkey baster, and, in just a few minutes, people hear him play Mozart on forty-seven brandy snifters filled with water. It's no gimmick. Jay Brown's instrument was once more popular than the piano. It is called the glass harp, and its music was once a favorite in the courts of kings.

Benjamin Franklin invented the glass harp; Mozart and Beethoven wrote pieces for it. Its sounds were so lovely and haunting that Franklin's pal, Dr. Franz Anton Mesmer, used it to hypnotize people.

"You play the thing," says Brown, "simply by rubbing wet fingers, human flesh, on glass."

He demonstrated, skating his fingers across the rims of the glass like a musical Hans Brinker.

The young performer resurrected the tinkling water bowls despite a curse fit for a pharaoh.

"The Franklin model," says Brown, "was forbidden in some cities. It was deadly. Players developed strange nervous disorders."

The Franklin bowls were colored with lead paint. That paint, seeping through the skin of the fingers, could have attacked the nervous system. The music of the glass harp faded, leaving only a sense of intrigue.

Three years ago, Brown, a professor and conductor of the Florida Philharmonic, rediscovered the ancient music. He bought lead-free glasses and began to teach.

"One of the great things about this instrument," says Brown, "no one comes away unhappy after listening to it. It brings out something bright. People feel like children facing a new world."

Jay Brown's quest for the perfect note is endless. He constantly searches for just the right glass, testing all kinds in department stores, in shopping centers, and at dinner parties.

Crystal is too costly and tends to ring too long. Jelly glasses are too thick.

"But all the notes are out there," says Brown, waving his hand at the shelves of glassware in a grocery store, "and I'll find them—if the Muzak isn't too loud."

The glass harp. Uniquely American. Just a set of water glasses. A common thing—in which Jay Brown saw a dream.

SIX

Goin' Back

". . . plucked out of the fields in time"
JIMMY DRIFTWOOD

Ozark Music

There has been a great revival of old-time music in the Ozarks. Folk festivals are now as familiar as the falling leaves.

It's hard to remember a time when music was not in these trees, but there was a moment when the music almost faded—like the leaves.

This is a hard land: only the strong and stubborn reap its harvest.

Jimmy Driftwood grew up here. He was a farmer who also taught history. Each evening as the sun slipped over the ridge, Jimmy Driftwood set his history lessons to song. One of them lifted him out of a tiny school in Snowball, Arkansas, and made him famous. "The Battle of New Orleans," which he wrote for his students, was recorded by country singer Johnny Horton and sold nine million records. It led to a national recording contract.

Driftwood became a star in the Grand Ole Opry and won

three Grammy awards. But back home, the hills were quiet. People no longer thought that their music mattered. It was that simple and that sad.

"Other sounds had come in," says Jimmy, "and the people were hearing the 'new' music. A lot of people felt like what they had always sung, people didn't care about or they'd be hearing it on radio and TV."

Jimmy Driftwood came home, determined to collect the old tunes and forgotten people before they were gone. His real life's work, he decided, was in the hills.

"I always had this dream," he says. "I wondered what had happened to all the old music and all the old songs and all the old tales, the old dances they used to do around my home. I guess my roots was in the Ozarks, and I wanted to come back."

Jimmy tramped the hills, tracking performers to their special places, where their music came easy, and coaxing them into town, where their old fingers could chase down chords for those who were eager to learn.

Every Friday and Saturday night, those who remembered the old songs—the farmers and the timber cutters—came to his barn. They came for the friendship . . . came back to help each other find the missing notes.

"I'm still a schoolteacher, really I am," he says as he watches his barn begin to fill. "Any time I've got an audience, if I don't teach them something, I should not have been there. Furthermore, if I don't learn something, I shouldn't be there."

Jimmy has gathered the words to eighteen hundred songs. He has heard snatches of more than three thousand tunes. At the age of seventy-seven, he is working against the clock to get them all down on paper.

"Some people are forgotten for periods of time," he says, "and some people are forgotten, period."

From inside the barn, there is a roar of laughter. Two old performers are racing each other to the end of a song.

"I think there's a certain quality about a music people play because they love to, rather than because they're being paid for it," he says.

Most nights when the neighbors pass the hat, they make barely enough to help Jimmy pay the light bill.

"I don't come for the money," says a small man with a harmonica. "I don't care if I get any money or not. I told them that. I just wanted to play."

Children no longer belittle the old music as they once did. Granny gowns and deck shoes go together naturally.

"People are going to have music one way or the other," says Jimmy. He puts a small hickory leaf in his mouth and begins to play a tune.

"If they don't have an instrument, they're going to make one. And if they have to, they'll play a leaf on a tree."

A mother shifts her child on her knees. The audience in the barn, now filled to capacity, is clapping, keeping time.

Jimmy Driftwood and friends

"I think many of the dreams are back home." he says. "I think people go a long way off, and then they come back and find it right here, at home."

Jimmy Driftwood has had a full harvest. His barn is filled with tunes that were plucked out of the fields in time.

A Dream Can Be
Under Your Feet

LEJUNIOR, KENTUCKY
(1982)

The mayor stood in the street. His high-topped shoes were covered with mud. He pointed to the deserted buildings.

"This was once a fine little town."

The year was 1964. Hellier, Kentucky, was closing.

"Down here we had a soda fountain, we had a dentist office, used-clothing stores. We had a nice little bank, an emergency hospital. Over that bridge came five to six trains a day."

Those statistics are but the clothes and the buttons of the place.

"We got six in this family!" shouted a welfare worker. "Let's load them up!"

People were leaving. The town's coal mine had been boarded up. It had sapped their spirit and had stung their souls.

Too tired and too broke, but stubborn and strong, the people moved on. They followed thousands of other out-of-work coal miners to the big auto plants up in the North. They had heard that life would have a happy ending there. That, too, melted away.

A generation later, the big car companies would lay off thousands of Appalachian workers. Many who had been set adrift in the 1950s would come back to a new boom in the coal industry and find jobs.

In 1974, Brenda Brock returned to see the mountains her parents had left when they followed the "better life" to Michigan. She had come to say good-bye to her grandparents. She planned to move to California and figured that if she lived so far away, she might never see her grandparents again.

"I had no intention of staying here," she said. She was sitting in her living room next to a big picture window that had a view of the setting sun in the valley beyond. "I've seen the ugliness that my mom and dad talked about. And yet, you get here and lose your heart."

She looked out the window at the burnt-orange mountains.

"Sometimes, I would sit in the city, and I couldn't even see the sky. That was the most depressing thing to me. I couldn't imagine how people lived their whole life and never looked up and seen the things that I see here every day."

Brenda really didn't long for another place. She longed for something within herself that she did not have—peace, solitude, a slower pace. Three years later she seized fate by the throat. Brenda Brock went looking for a job in the coal mines. She showed up hungry and broke on a mine foreman's doorstep. All she had was a sleeping bag. Her parents thought she was crazy.

"They asked me why," she said. "And I even wondered why. Why am I here? How did I end up here? My parents can't understand why I would want to come back to what they escaped from. But this is my spot."

Her work below was a trade-off for her life above. Today there are three thousand women in the coal mines doing virtually every tough, grimy job. When Brenda got a job, she called home and asked her younger sister, Tammy, to join her underground. She did. They now make more than their parents did on the auto assembly lines, but their new-found prosperity has not put them on easy street.

The morning I arrived, the coal furnace in the home they share had broken for the third time in as many weeks. They were trying to fix it. Outside, it was twenty degrees.

"Push some of that coal back," said Brenda. She grabbed an iron poker from a bucket next to the heater. "The motor's going to burn up."

Tammy raced outside to look at the chimney.

"If it was clogged," she yelled, "it wouldn't be coming out of the hole."

Brenda opened the furnace door and stuck a flashlight into the smoke.

"Can't see nothing," she called out. "I'll shut 'er off."

Brenda's baby, sixteen-month-old Israel, had been playing on a blanket spread out on the floor. She carried her next to the stove in the kitchen, then went back for Tammy's five-month-old Shasta. The sisters are raising their children alone.

Brenda has worked in the mines for five years. Worked even when she was seven months pregnant.

"I wasn't nervous about going underground," she said as we worked on the furnace motor. "I was nervous because, well, all of the men. There's a superstition that women bring bad luck in a mine. For a long time, the men kept saying, 'They're going to fool around and they're going to hire a bunch of women in here and they're going to get us everyone killed.' And the men kept saying that and saying that. Nobody never did get killed. Nobody never did get hurt in my mine, but it frightened me."

A single church bell echoed through the valley. Far off, six men struggled up a steep hill. They were pulling a pine box.

Sadness seeped down the mountains.

Twenty-two people had died in the coal fields near Brenda that winter.

"I was never, ever afraid to go underground until I had my

baby," she says. "I was never afraid. Then, all of a sudden, when I had my baby, I was terrified to be there. All I could think about was that I was all she had."

"How did you overcome that fear?" I asked.

"I couldn't let it overcome me because then it would have ended us both."

Snow began to fall. Brenda reached down and lifted her child into her arms. She pointed to a faraway mountain.

"See right up there? Right there?"

The baby followed her finger.

"Up there on the mountain? Sometime, when you get a little bit bigger, and you can help mommy, we're going to build us a house 'way up there."

Israel looked back at her mother. Her voice sounded like a lullaby. She blinked and sleepily nodded her head.

"We're going to have us a swing and a teeter-totter and all kinds of things," Brenda cooed.

"If the coal boom ends," I asked, "would you move on like your dad did?"

Brenda rocked a moment, then said, "I don't think so. I really feel like this is where my heart is. This is my home."

The baby was asleep.

"I'll probably never leave here. I'll build here. I'll stay here. I'll grow here to be an old lady."

The Hermit Engineer

EIGHT DOLLAR MOUNTAIN, OREGON
(1980)

Eight Dollar Mountain, Oregon, is where the redwoods trail away north of the California border, and the clouds creep among the pine trees. For centuries, the sea winds played the only music on this mountain. That was before Paul Lutus moved here. At thirty-four Paul Lutus wanted to get away from it all, while taking it all with him. He built a cabin in the wilderness with no running water, no telephone—just a cat for company. A cat and a computer. Lutus wanted to see if he could work as well in the woods as he did in the city. Well, he worked better.

The young computer programmer was a consultant for NASA before he went into the wilderness. He helped get the Viking space probe to Mars. In his tiny shack, miles from the nearest road, Lutus created a new lighting system that is now part of the space shuttle and he found a way for folks to make a quick sketch of their dream house, then see it instantly in three dimensions, from any angle. How does the world get in touch with Paul Lutus?

"One guy flew over on a hang glider," he said. "He dropped a rock on my roof. I knew I had company."

Pals do stop by. Now that Paul has programmed his computer to play music, electronic concerts echo down the canyon walls. Friends bring their own instruments and join in.

"A computer never takes a breath," Lutus explained, "so it's hard to play along."

Nobody brings a cello. Paul's home is 450 feet straight up. Picking your way hand over hand along a forest path is the only way to get there. So far, only piccolo players and bill collectors have made it to his door.

"Why do you make it so tough for folks to come see you?" I asked.

"Oh, I don't make it difficult at all," said Lutus. His round wire-rimmed glasses reflected in the computer screen and gave

Paul Lutus with his musical computer

him the look of a scholar. It was evening. The cabin was lit by a single kerosene lamp. His cat was curled up next to the keyboard.

"It's very easy," he tapped a computer key. "All they have to do is go to the end of the highway, come out on the dirt road that is washed out. Drive to the end. Stop and get out of the car. Walk about two miles. Come up the hill in the dark, in the rain with their flashlights, and I always welcome them, if they have a lot of wine and firewood."

Lutus grinned and turned back to the computer screen. I glanced around. Everything in his cabin—his bed, his table, the cast-iron stove—he had hauled up that trail outside.

"I've constantly been escalating what I could carry. I just carried a couch up," Lutus said when he had finished. "It was great fun.

"This couch is about five feet long, and it weighs somewhere about two hundred pounds. I purchased it and put it in my truck. Drove over here. Put it down on the ground and tied a back pack to it so I'd have a real support system for it. I tied a lot of ropes around the couch and then sat down and put the backpack on my shoulders.

"I couldn't get up, couldn't get it off the ground. So I got out of the backpack, put it up on the back of the truck. It was about hip level. Then I walked back into the straps and walked forward. The whole four hundred feet of the mountain, I was going, 'If I fall down, this is going to be awful.'

"The couch was about three feet over my head, swaying back and forth and catching branches and things. It was raining. I managed not to fall over. That was great fun!"

Lutus built his treetop house by hand. It took 150 trips to carry up the lumber. He finished the job in twenty days.

"You have to nail quick or the logs'll roll down the hill," he joked.

Four times a week, Paul runs down the mountain for water, then pulls his way back. He said he lives this way because it's good exercise.

You wouldn't expect to find a space-age scientist out here, but then nothing Paul Lutus has done is ordinary. He dropped out of school in the seventh grade to study electronics and astronomy. He was a successful TV repairman at twelve, a medical researcher and a chief engineer at eighteen. Now, Lutus lives on forty dollars a month, which includes the electric bill. The rest of his money is spent on computers. He has brought twelve thousand dollars worth of gear to the top of his mountain.

"There are a lot of professions that are better served by living out in the country," said Lutus. "A lot of creative endeavors don't survive big cities. Potted plants outside windows and computer programmers both wither away in town."

"When you decided to build your house up here, you obviously had to give a lot of thought to what you would take up," I concluded. "Is there something you decided you just couldn't carry?"

He pondered for a moment, then said, "There was something once. It was big and heavy. I was going to build an observatory for my telescope out of cinder blocks, and I changed my mind about that.

"I have never encountered something that I couldn't bring up here that I really needed. There are things I decided I didn't need."

"Like what?" I asked.

"A road."

"Where I Knew I Belonged"

Americans have always been dreamers in the woods. In times of trouble, we turn to the wilderness for comfort. Back in the 1960s and 1970s, a whole wave of folks stopped what they were doing and went looking for wilderness. We called them "dropouts." But that missed the mark by a country mile.

Josh Powell is typical of the thousands who turned their backs on high-rise careers.

He was born in the Kentucky hill country and raised on a farm. He worked his way through law school in Atlanta, landed a job with one of the town's best-known firms, then gave it all up to run a one-man sawmill.

"I came from the country," says Powell. "I spent the first eighteen years of my life in the country. I really yearned to get back to the place where I knew I belonged. The ten months that I spent downtown in Atlanta, I spent a lot of time thinking.

"I said, 'You know, there's some young man who really needs

this office and really wants it. And here I am, a young man who doesn't need it, and doesn't want it.' So I left. I hadn't been gone fifteen minutes 'til a young gentleman took my desk. Now he's a partner in that law firm, and he's happy. And, Lord knows, I am."

Josh Powell is a self-appointed inspector of sunsets. In Atlanta he missed the slight sounds of evening that lifted his spirits. He wanted his daughter to live in a place where one life is still threaded to another.

Powell bought twenty-four acres in the wilderness of north Georgia. He worked alone and built himself a house that his wife designed from a picture they had seen on a paint can. Powell had never worked with wood before. He was not a carpenter. When he made a mistake, he simply cut down another tree and started over. Building that house, Josh Powell fell in love with his tiny sawmill. His courtroom battles were behind him. The forest never argued.

"To speak to a tree and know it doesn't speak back," says Powell, "is worth a whole lot."

Powell and his wife, Ann, found that they could live just as well on less. Josh did not make as much money as he once had, but neighbors were eager to trade for his services.

Was it difficult to give up the security of a well-paying job?

"No," he says. "I think there is no security. The problem with security is you know that that's all you have. And you know that is what it's going to be. And you know what is going to be at the end of the month, and what's going to be after that. I find a whole lot more fun in getting out and seeing if you can make it on your own."

The Powells never did drop out. Ann Powell teaches math at a nearby college. Josh works long and hard, like a man whose horizons are never quite at his elbows. That was something his father simply did not understand.

"I did a cruel thing," says Powell. "I took my dad downtown to the office where I had been and rode him in their magnificent elevator. He stepped off on those thick rugs. And he saw the antiques in the reception room, and he walked down the hall. And he saw all these men in suits. And he never could understand how in the world anybody could give that up and come out here and do something like this. Well, he came from that generation when things weren't that way. He farmed because he had to. I saw wood because I want to."

Joe Clark

CUMBERLAND GAP, TENNESSEE
(1980)

It's appropriate that this story about going home is set here in
Cumberland Gap. Most of America passed through this break in
the mountains a couple of centuries ago—leaving home, looking
for new lives. Folks around here like to remember Daniel Boone
and Abe Lincoln and all the other famous people who passed this
way. But a fellow by the name of Joe Clark thinks that the
people who stayed are just as important. They planted the roots
of his childhood and gave him a place to come home to.

Joe Clark left this valley forty years ago. He carried with him
pictures of friends and neighbors who would set a course for his
life. Joe went to work for the great news magazines, *Time* and
Life and *Newsweek*, capturing the face of the common man. But
he never forgot those first pictures or the friends who inspired
them.

Seasons, like signposts, mark the time. In the fall of his
seventy-sixth year, Joe Clark decided to come back to Cumber-

land Gap for a harvest of memory. The faces he found were much the same; only the generations had changed.

Thirty years earlier, Joe Clark had taken pictures of his neighbors performing what he thought was the last of an old-time harvest ritual, farm families gathering together to boil down cane syrup to make molasses. It was more than just ritual; it was the height of the social season.

"Teenagers would go courtin' in the woods around the fire," Clark recalls, "and little chaperones in pigtails would keep an eye on their big brothers and sisters. They would report their activity to the community at large."

Clark's eyes twinkle in the firelight.

"You know," he continues, "in some places, America as it used to be still is."

He moves off through the clearing, snapping pictures.

"If you want to go after the wonderment of life," he says, "take your camera and go home. It's not the people in China or

Making molasses

on the other side of the world. The most wonderful people in the world are right in your own backyard."

Children are dipping cane stalks into vats of boiling molasses. A hot, gooey stream of sugar runs down one boy's cheek.

"When I was a kid," says Clark, "we didn't fight germs, we et 'em—alive."

It was something more than nostalgia that brought Joe Clark back to the cane patch this cold autumn night.

"My blood turned as blue as the icy rain!"

Clark sits in a crowd of kids.

"Ole Trouble kept moving up the mountain."

He is weaving a tall tale.

When Joe Clark was a boy, there were ghosts in these fields, and old-time storytellers told their listeners to keep their little eyes peeled. He worries, now that the old storytellers are gone, if the place hasn't lost some of its magic.

He doesn't need to fret. He has brought his own.

Singles' Lawman

DALLAS, TEXAS
(1981)

The good life, Texas style: a singles' complex so big it has twenty-six swimming pools and pulls its own television shows in from satellites. Four hundred acres of lakes and jogging trails spread out over the prairie right in the heart of Texas. It is called The Village, a small city, really—ten thousand single adults, half of them in their early twenties, hardly anyone over thirty-four— young, good-looking, well-off.

Unfortunately, the things that make them happy also make them prime targets for crime. During one month, there were twenty-seven daylight burglaries. Seventeen rapes in one year.

What to do? Well remember, folks, this is Texas. The Village did what a town's got to do—it went looking for a lawman on horseback.

Since Dave Moore took over the job, only two burglars have gotten away.

"The horse," says Moore, "is an observation platform that

comes through these parking lots and in between these buildings and upstairs and downstairs with no headlights and no engine noise. He is very effective."

Because of Moore's perch and unobstructed view, daytime burglaries dropped 90 percent in one month.

"The burglars just went someplace else," says Moore, standing in his stirrups to see over a hedge.

Tenants who have trouble relating to a cop in a car will talk to a man on horseback.

"I know a guy that has a key that will open any apartment," says a woman jogger, who has stopped to pat Moore's horse.

"You do?" asks Moore.

"Yes. What's your horse's name?"

"Smitty."

Smitty is a terrific detective. So is Moore.

Moore is not a cowboy by profession. He spent six years in the military police before taking to the saddle. He now covers fifty miles a day, sidestepping sunbathers and joggers across the Texas range.

What does he handle that John Wayne did not?

"Pool complaints. Loud stereos. Domestic disturbances. Parking violations."

Moore finishes scribbling the information from the woman jogger in his notebook. A sports car skids past in the parking lot.

"Concrete. John Wayne never had to deal with concrete."

Three girls approach with a can of orange drink.

"This is really Texas," one girl giggles, "to see a horse at The Village."

"Can Smitty have a sip?"

Moore nods.

The girl lifted the can.

"He prefers grape soda," says Moore.

They all laugh.

"The first horse we had was still a little spooky when he came out here," says patrol manager Jim Nelson. "He was tied to a flagpole. Reared back, broke his reins, and fell over the hood of a car. His saddle horn went through the windshield. The horse made a nice fourteen-hundred-pound dent."

Smitty's care and feeding is less than half the cost of a security car. He has proved so successful, other complexes in Dallas are now looking into getting their own horse patrols. The horse is quick, quiet, and cheap—and can get more places than a car.

"Oh, just one thing," says Moore, turning Smitty into the sunset.

"What's that?"

"Watch out for their exhaust."

Mom-and-Pop Jail

Not so long ago, every town had a mom-and-pop grocery store. Tourists stayed in private houses. Main streets were family-owned and family-run until one by one they were replaced by shopping malls and motels. Local landmarks are all that remain to distinguish one main street from another.

In Danville, Pennsylvania, there is an old Victorian house across from a neighborhood church. It is the last mom-and-pop operation in town.

Fred and Gloria Shepperson live there. They have a teenage daughter and a teenage son and they take in some "boarders" to help make ends meet. The Sheppersons live in the front half of their old Victorian house. The boarders live in the back.

"Morning, Steamboat," says Fred, calling through a thick iron door.

"Morning, Sheriff," comes a voice from the other side.

Fred and Gloria run Pennsylvania's last mom-and-pop jail.

206

"Five dollars and ninety cents for five boxes of cereal," Fred complains, sitting at the kitchen table. "It ought to have gold nuggets in it for that kind of money."

"It's not so bad," says Gloria, stirring thick pots of soup on her stove. "I come from a large family, twelve children. All you do is add a few more potatoes in the pot, a little broth, and you have it made."

The inmates eat what the Sheppersons eat. Gloria cooks on the weekends, but, like any other working mom, there are times when the family must fend for itself.

" Who wants to go out for Kentucky Fried Chicken this evening?" yells one of the inmates.

A dozen hands in a dozen cells go up.

"Anybody ever try to escape from this jail?" I ask.

"Yeah," says Sheriff Shepperson. "We had a guy who noticed the floors had some enormous cracks. He'd be out in the hall in front of his cell every morning working on them. It kept him busy and occupied during the day. This went on for about four or five weeks. Then I went back to him one night at lockup time and said, 'There's no sense continuing digging anymore, because after you get through the concrete, you got the three-quarter-inch steel plate and then you got your brick under that, and then you're going to end up in the basement. You can't go nowhere anyway.'

Relatives like the little jail in the neighborhood. They get to see the inmates more often. For some folks, the place is downright romantic.

"Let me get this straight," I ask Steamboat's woman friend on visiting day. "You started going together *after* he came here?"

She smiles and holds the inmate's hand.

"You might say we got a little closer. I drop by a lot, and he's never stood me up yet."

The jail houses only men. The Sheppersons' daughter, Pam, wasn't too happy about moving in.

"Sure, I was scared," says Pam. "I was really scared. I didn't know what to expect."

Her folks solved the problem by giving her the room farthest from the cells.

Now it is one big family here in the neighborhood pokey. And the inmates, while not completely happy, seem to appreciate that.

"I like the food here," says Steamboat, who is serving sixty days for shooting out streetlights. "It's yummy."

He looks past the bars to where the sheriff is making his evening rounds.

"Be it ever so humble," he mumbles.

"Good night, Steamboat," says the Sheriff.

"Good night, Sheriff."

Sailing Cargo

Success is not a harbor but a voyage that ripples and twists, shifting imperceptibly back over courses already charted.

Sailboats on the Chesapeake Bay wait for Sunday sailors, but there was a time when ships chased and caught the wind for profit, carrying cargo to the world.

Although it seems impossible, some sailing craft can actually go faster than the speed of wind. An iceboat with minimal friction can go four times as fast.

In recent years, some people have questioned our traditional ways of catching the wind at sea. One designer wants to build ships not with sails, but with windmills to power the propellers. The Japanese have launched an oil tanker that runs with wind. And, in Norfolk harbor, there's a tugboat unlike any ever seen before.

"We're getting some wind out there now, Virginia!" yells

the captain, poking his pipe out the wheelhouse window. "Back off, Jesse!"

He is piloting a Tugantine—part tugboat, part sailboat.

"What d'ya say there, Cap?" sings back the deckhand.

"Haul away!"

The Tugantine started as a joke, a way for Captain Lane Briggs to enter a sailing regatta, but when he noticed a 28 percent saving in fuel, the sails stayed on.

"There's lots of people who refer to us as nuts," says Briggs. "The only thing I can say is, she's making her bank payments."

The tug slides away into the breeze.

"You don't catch us running up and down the bay, tacking back and forth with a barge behind us. The engine is still our main source of power, but when the wind's in our favor, we use sail. We've been able to use it on the average of 50 to 60 percent of the time."

Briggs leans out of the window in the pilothouse to check the sheets.

"This country was discovered under sail," he says, pulling his pipe from his mouth. "All our freight and commodity was carried many years under sail. What drove it out was cheap fuel. Now fuel is got high, plus scarce. So we're going to have to do something to come back and offset some of that."

Up the Chesapeake Bay near Deltaville, Virginia, Joe Spivey built a two-masted cargo schooner when the price of diesel fuel rose tenfold in the past decade. He runs an inboard motor when he must, but the silent press of wind on sail keeps his bottom line afloat.

"We felt like we had to go with something that was proven," says Spivey, "something that we knew would work. Something that had been used commercially and had been used successfully commercially."

The schooner captain makes a good living with a ship whose basic design has not changed since the turn of the century.

"The development of cargo sailing ships took hundreds of years, and it would seem silly to throw all that knowledge away," says Spivey.

In the Bahamas, Spivey had watched small boats shuttling canned goods for huge profits. Figured he could do the same in this country, if he could keep costs down. Old sailing captains showed him how. Spivey's wife, Sharon, stitched the sails. They sold the family farm to finance the operation.

"I'm a businessman. I'm not a dreamer," says Spivey, who graduated with a degree in economics from Virginia Commonwealth University. "We've done our research. We've done the market study. We've taken the time to really check the market out."

But the couple was soon faced with an unforeseen problem. The Coast Guard had no category for motorized sailing ships, and the ancient design that put them in business was barnacled with legislation unchanged since the age of sail.

The Spiveys' decision to have an inboard engine was the sticking point.

"The Coast Guard rules and regulations don't fit us," Spivey says glumly. "As far as they're concerned, you're either a sailboat or a motor boat."

Ironically, if Spivey had taken out his ship's engine, he could have been fully licensed. But the motor keeps him safe and his cargo on schedule.

The couple thought about leaving the country and flying a foreign flag but decided to stay and fight to change the law. Joe has testified several times before a Congressional subcommittee studying the problem. Congress has not ruled. The Coast Guard has allowed the Spiveys to operate while the law is under review.

"This is the real world," says Joe. "You can't run away. It's like on board my ship. When the rain comes down and the wind is in your teeth, you have to get up, even though you don't feel like it, and take in sail and take care of the boat.

"You can't call in sick from the real world."

SEVEN

I Won't Grow Up!

"My father loves children. He wishes I had been one."
AMY DOTSON, AGE SIX

The Boys of Winter

Dawn in St. Petersburg, Florida. The fishermen are already in place. It's a big day for Fred Broadwell. He's about to make a comeback. Fred Broadwell is a baseball player. A couple of seasons ago, he was sidelined with pneumonia. Now he is back at age ninety-five.

"Play ball!"

"Hit one, Freddy! Swing!"

The old man waits for the pitch. He doesn't crouch over the strike zone. He leans into the wind, seemingly suspended. The ball floats toward the plate. Freddy stings it toward the short-stop and takes off toward first base.

"Go, Freddy!"

The shortstop stabs at the ball, fielding it on one hop, then stops. His back is stiff. The third baseman grabs the ball from the shortstop's glove and arcs it across the diamond.

Freddy beats the throw by a step.

Freddy at the bat

All in a day's play. Nobody on this ball field is under seventy-five. The two teams, called the Kids and the Kubs, have battled each other every winter, three days a week, sixty games a year, for half a century.

When these fellows talk about the great old players, they don't mean DiMaggio, Gehrig, or Ruth; they're talking about guys like Ed Forrest, who stood on his head at home plate to celebrate his eightieth birthday. And Charles Eldridge, who took up the game at age one hundred. And Chappy Chapman, who hit 144 times in one year. Chappy still circles the bases faster than the scorekeeper can keep score.

George Bakewell was the oldest member of the club before Fred Broadwell made his comeback. Now there's something of a friendly competition. Ten times a day, George jogs up the stairs in his retirement home. He jumps rope a couple of dozen times a day, just to get his blood pumping. Fred prefers another method. He likes to walk with the ladies. George swings a six-pound iron pipe before each game. Fred lifts nothing heavier than a twelve-ounce beer can.

The Three-Quarter Century Club is something of an institution in St. Petersburg. It's got more tradition than a Japanese sumo wrestler. Before each game, the players march the base paths, salute the flag, and repeat the club cheer, "What's the matter with seventy-five, we're the boys that's still alive. Hi-Ho. Let's Go. Rah! Rah! Seventy-five!"

Every three days or so, whenever one side begins to score more than the other, club officials get together and trade players to keep the games even. Fred used to play third base. He now plays short center field, where the balls come slower, and the throws aren't quite so far. Everybody plays whatever position he feels up to that day.

When they are not on the field, players pass among the fans, selling programs and kisses. George Bakewell is the club historian. He writes of days long ago and triple plays, and he entertains the crowd with his poetry.

> "Backwards, turn backwards, oh,
> Time on your flight.
> Make me a boy again for just one
> night.
> The spirit is willing, let's go all
> out.
> The flesh says, 'Hold it, Daddy.
> Remember your arthritis, lumbago, and
> your gout.' "

The first set of ground rules made fifty years ago called for the batter to walk, not run to first base. City officials in St. Petersburg were concerned that the players would have heart attacks. And, some of them have.

"Four years ago," says Bakewell, "I was coaching on first base, and Morrison, the first baseman, reached up to get the ball and fell over dead in my arms."

He demonstrates, then dusts himself off.

"That's a nice way to go. You can't beat that. I'll take that anytime."

In the midst of winter, these fellows have found an invincible summer.

Crack!

A roar goes up from the crowd. The ball dribbles through the right fielder's legs. Old Freddy shuffles toward home plate. George Bakewell starts yelling.

"How's that for a ninety-five-year-old man?"

Freddy doffs his hat as he passes home plate.

"They can't throw out a ninety-five-year-old man!" cries George.

Sometimes there's just no substitute for experience.

The Flying Fathers

DEEP RIVER, ONTARIO, CANADA
(1979)

Morning mass in Deep River, Canada. Nothing unusual, really—except, gathered in this chapel are priests who have seen every Pat O'Brien movie ever made. They are more than just priests. They are a team. Out of clerical garb and on the ice, they are known as the Flying Fathers, one of the best hockey squads in North America. They play anyone, anywhere, for charity and children. In eighteen years, they have lost only five games.

How do they win so many games? They cheat. The Flying Fathers are not above distracting the referee while putting Plexiglas in front of the net to keep the other team from scoring. They have been known to lasso opposing goalies with a twelve-foot rosary. The penalty: two minutes in the confessional box for playing like a Protestant. If a player still manages to score against them, the priests recruit him on the spot with a cape, a candle, a "Hail Mary"—and a pail of holy water in the face.

The captain of the Flying Fathers is a Canadian priest working in Detroit. The rest live in Canada. Some played professional hockey before joining the priesthood. All moonlight with the team as often as they can.

Their leader, Father Vaughan Quinn, O.M.I., is not the kind of guy you might expect—quiet and inspirational. He wears a beany and carries a teddy bear. When Father Quinn is not playing hockey, he drives a fire truck. On sunny days, you can see the good father racing his fire engine through stoplights in Detroit, hauling gangs of alcoholics who have never learned how to enjoy life sober. Father Quinn runs the largest alcoholic rehabilitation center in the Midwest. The fire engine is part of the therapy, teaching drunks to have fun without drink.

Those who fall off his wagon are likely to end up in Father Quinn's 1925 Dodge hearse. He doesn't wait until a man is dead.

Sister Mary Shooter

He saves him from the sidewalk. The hearse is Father Quinn's drunk tank.

The good Father was once a drunk himself. That's why the priests take their fun so seriously. It is their way of reaching folks. Church attendance soars when the Flying Fathers come to town.

"You can't stay in the rectory," says Quinn, "and wait for folks to come to you. People come up to us after every game and talk hockey. And then some of them say, 'Hey, I could use some help.'"

The crowd roars and jumps to its feet. Father Quinn has skated onto the ice holding the tail of a horse named Penance. He was chasing the Flying Fathers' best player, a priest disguised as a nun named "Sister Mary Shooter." They race down the ice and jump on the other team's goalie. When the snow has cleared, there are four pucks in the net.

I'm not sure the scholars of Rome would understand all this, but "Sister Mary Shooter" does. You gotta be folks to touch folks.

Pirate

To all of us who grew up watching Errol Flynn reruns, this place is kind of special. Beaufort, North Carolina, used to be a safe harbor for pirates. Blackbeard had a home just off the main street. There were more parrots and eye patches on these wharves than on the MGM back lot. And there still are.

"Pipe me aboard, Mr. Brown!"

Meet the master of the *Meka II*.

"Look lively, mates!"

His name is Ross Morphew.

"Jump! Jump!"

His crew calls him Sinbad.

"If you dare get my coat the least bit wet, I'll have you on the yardarm."

Sinbad runs the only school for pirates this side of Hollywood.

222

Classes include Swashbuckling 101, Cannon Firing, and Remedial Rowing.

Teenagers pay eighty dollars a day to race the waves, searching for something they do not possess: on these decks, they can be heroes.

"Sure we've got our astronauts and our medical heroes," says Sinbad. "Sometimes it's hard to relate to them; they're so sophisticated. It's easier to be a pirate."

Sinbad was born, if not three centuries too late, then at least three decades. He would have been perfect at Republic Studios. His advanced students are given training in abducting fair maidens. If they happen to be fair maidens, a fair master will do.

Sinbad takes his students to a place where all the clocks have stopped and the images have a heartbeat of their own.

"There's nothing like going to sea and being out of sight of land for seven or eight days. You can't see a thing, and you're doing all the navigating by the stars and the sun and the moon. You're really not sure of your position. All of a sudden, there it is," says Sinbad. He looks past his students to some invisible horizon. "The island you've been looking for. You can't express it. It's just, well," he pauses, "you did it yourself."

Sinbad built his ship from an old English blueprint, built it with his own hands in his backyard in Michigan.

"I was working for General Motors. My neighbors knew I had this dream. They said I could build the ship, but when it dwarfed their homes, they tossed me out. I trucked her down to the Detroit River, and set sail."

Sinbad is serious about his school, but his piracy is basically laid back.

"We're going to attack ship as soon as I finish my sandwich."

It is graduation day, and the class is swooping into Beaufort harbor for a final exam.

"Blast 'em!"

All the students need is a sound track. They are armed with a thousand water balloons, which they toss at anyone in sight.

SEVEN: I Won't Grow Up!

People fight back, but buckets and garden hoses are no match for water bombs.

It is not difficult to understand how Sinbad can capture a child's imagination. He is part of the adventure that built this country. And all of us, no matter how far removed from childhood dreams, can still thrill to those who live them.

Circus Children

There is something to be said for summertime in a small town. The circus still comes in a tent. There aren't many circuses left that stretch their big tops like the imagination. Perhaps that's why the ones that do, go to so many places. For the Carson and Barnes Circus, Wewoka, Oklahoma, is the seventieth city in seventy days. For the kids who tuck under the tent flap, it is always the first time.

What is it about the circus that tickles the memory? I remember my first. There was a seventy-six-year-old lion and tiger trainer, billed as the "Oldest Living Lion and Tiger Trainer in the World." Years later, I had the opportunity to ask the trainer how he kept his job.

"Simple," he said. "I taught all my cats in Spanish, French, and Cherokee. No one wants to do this job holding a dictionary!"

Most of the families in the Carson and Barnes Circus have been doing what they are doing for eight generations—father to son, son to his son. Education is immediate, important, and no one can convince the children it isn't fun. Five days a week, fifty weeks a year, the circus kids follow the big top to their one-room schoolhouse in the cook tent. Their teacher, Faye Reynolds, works the class like a ringmaster.

"Table two, start your reading assignment. Table five, keep counting."

Their education is practical. The older kids learn how to fill out life insurance forms.

"Who's working the big cats this afternoon?" asks Mrs. Reynolds.

Two boys raise their hands.

"Take a minimum deduction."

The children all laugh.

There are thirteen kids in the class, kindergarten to college. Geography is taught using a map of their travels.

"The things that other kids may have to read in a book," says Mrs. Reynolds, "these kids have seen."

Each season brings a twenty-thousand-mile field trip. While town kids come to see the circus, circus children go see the towns.

Faye Reynolds gave up a teaching job in Illinois just six years short of retirement to follow this life. So did her husband, Wayne. He now plays trombone in the circus band. Her two grown sons came along, too. One blows a tuba, and the other, Bill, directs the band. Bill's wife, Jeanie, was a social worker before she joined.

"Well, I must tell you," she says, "I had never seen a circus until I met Bill."

What is the lure of this kind of life?

"We have itchy feet," says Wayne, "and this is a good way to keep 'em scratched."

Faye's granddaughter sits in a playpen next to the band-stand while her dad directs the Grand Entry and her mom curls up in an elephant's trunk. You have to wonder what's left to amaze a baby like that, growing up under a traveling big top.

Jeanie Reynolds says, "Just one thing. When I took her into a house for the first time, she said, 'Wow, Mama! This is big!' "

She wondered how many trucks it would take to pull that thing.

Marbles

Okay, here's a little quiz. If a fellow's "lost all his marbles," but he's "playing for keeps," "shooting sticks," and "tossing boulders," what's going on?

If you can answer that, you're probably older than you want to be, or perhaps you've been through Naoma, West Virginia. Folks here "play for keeps" better than anyone else in the world. I'm talking marbles, and not the kind they use to make coffee tables.

Naoma is a marble shooter's Mecca. This little town has had four national and one world champion. Before a kid can tie his sneakers around here, he knows the joy of knuckles in the dirt.

For most of America, marbles died out with dime novels and Big Little Books, but here in this tiny mountain village, it is still a game that keeps everyone the same age.

I wanted to know how a town of five hundred people could

produce so many winners. I found the answer at Ray Jarrell's gas station.

Ray Jarrell is the dean of Naoma marble shooters. He won a national title in 1972 and became world champion two years later. He successfully defended his crown three times, then retired.

Jarrell has won twenty thousand marbles. After school and on weekends, kids gather above his grease rack to learn at the feet of a master.

"It was tough in school," says Jarrell. "Nobody would play me no marbles." He laughs. "At least not for keeps!"

Jarrell's approach to the game makes Minnesota Fats look like a missionary.

"With a lot of young kids, you can sit there and spin your marble. Jerk it as you flip and it will come back to you. The kids'll just sit there, cold-like, and say, 'Golly, how did he do that?'"

They also don't reckon with Ray Jarrell's secret weapon, so secret he keeps it enshrined in a cup of lard: a big orange shooting marble called Old Faithful. That shooter has won every tournament the town ever entered. Ray plans to pass it down to Billy Gloshen, age thirteen, the great new hope for Naoma. Billy's got the eye, the concentration, and a mom who doesn't care about grease stains.

I just couldn't leave without asking, "What do you champs eat for breakfast?"

They both answered in unison, "Eggs!"

Toy Museum

How many hours have we lingered by toy store windows? I suppose there's no more common way to mark the calendar of our lives. I came across a 1938 Superman doll the other day. It reminded me of how differently each generation views its heroes. In 1938, Superman would have sooner kissed a crate of kryptonite than Lois Lane.

Why do you suppose toys mean more to us as the years go by? Joe Daole should know. He's got a house filled with them—more than one hundred thousand. Many were handmade and reflect their time.

"They're not just playthings; they're memories," says Daole, dusting a porcelain Man-in-the-Moon who has yet to hear from mission control. A tiny Teddy Roosevelt is propped nearby, still looking for votes. To the side, a great column of toy soldiers is set out for war in front of a doll-size army barracks built from dynamite boxes sent back from the front by a father who wished he were home.

Joe Daole has collected all sorts of things all his life. When he was in the army, he filled his duffel bag with rare rocks instead of laundry. He buys a toy nearly every day. His collection is now worth more than one million dollars and is open for all to see in an old house on Peachtree Street in Atlanta.

"If I had to just collect and store these toys in boxes," says Daole, "I would have quit. There's no fun in looking at big storage boxes or brown paper bags.

"I can't paint, and I can't draw a straight line. I'm no artist, but I am showing people something that they can come and have for a couple of hours—a complete review of their youth."

Joe never restores a toy. The dents and the dust, he says, come naturally.

"It's been played with. It's been used, and it's been loved."

Toy soldiers poised before their barracks

SEVEN: I WON'T GROW UP!

The collector turns to show a toddler a tiny bear, and her joy shines in her eyes.

"It's rather sad to see a toy in the original box," he says. "You sort of feel the toy should have been handled just a little bit."

The child hugs the bear and dances away to a corner. Joe Daole smiles and returns to his dusting. It seems that the life of a toy collector, like the life of a gardener, must have built-in happiness. Those toys that are loved, have lasted, and their appeal is still special.

Papa Manteo

Did you know that some of our most cherished childhood stories started over a family argument? In 1719, there lived a printer who detested his mother-in-law. She was forever filling his baby's head with fairy tales. One evening, the printer got so annoyed that he stayed up all night and copied them down, and then he passed them around to the neighbors. It was an attempt to embarrass his mother-in-law. But the neighbors liked the tales of Mother Goose. Imagination never grows up.

Mike Manteo has held onto his childhood things. They hang in the dust-combed darkness of his Coney Island electrical shop.

"Good morning, my children," he says as he flicks on an overhead light. His nails are short and cracked. A wooden prince stares down at him. A wooden queen smiles benignly from beneath paint-chipped cheeks.

"How's your face? Is it dry?" "Papa" Manteo raises the visor on a knight's helmet, touches the face, then wipes his finger on his work pants. He is a small man, balding, but powerfully built. In the shadows, he could pass for Yogi Berra. He moves to the back of the shop. He is framed now by dozens of dangling life-sized marionettes. They are carved from solid oak; dressed in buffed brass. The last of their kind. Polished and lovingly repaired by a proud man who created through them the great adventure he dreamed for his own life.

As a boy, Mike Manteo would sit on a sand pail and watch his dad swing these huge dolls, teetering on his toes above a stage, creating great gulping moments of passion for the Italian immigrants who wanted a touch of home. His papa had brought the puppets from Sicily. They performed nightly soap operas, ancient tales of lust and romance and battle. Each story took more than a year to tell and played to packed houses at his father's theater on New York's Lower East Side.

Mike learned the Italian dialogue for all two hundred

Papa Manteo and his knight

marionettes, eventually working alongside his dad—eighteen hours a day, seven days a week, for twelve years.

"I was getting twenty-five cents a day," he says. "Sometimes I would tell him, 'Hey, Pa. Gee, what you going to do with twenty-five cents a day?'

" 'Why? What'sa matter?' " His father would explode. " 'Explain to me, what'sa matter.' " Mike changes his voice, imitating his dad.

" 'Well, gee, what can I do with twenty-five cents?' " He is performing now, waving his arms dramatically, " 'I can't even go to the movie.'

" 'How much is the movie?'

" 'Well, the movie's fifteen cents.' " Manteo puffs up, acting like his papa about to make a point. He pauses and stabs the air with his finger.

" 'You still got ten cents!' "

Mike took over the theater when his father retired. His sister, Aida, helped with the love scenes. Other brothers, cousins, and uncles worked backstage. The place continued to flourish.

A half century ago, radio began to send soap operas into the home—in English. The crowds, now more American than Italian, stopped coming. Papa Manteo's theater closed. The family drifted to other jobs. Mike put his father's marionettes away. Occasionally, he performed at a church or a school, but mostly the puppets sat, silent and sad.

After supper and on weekends, Mike would take one down, paint a new face, or carve a leg. Neighbors would leave broken toasters and teakettles for him to pound into shiny new armor. His sister, Aida, kept the marionettes fresh with elaborate costumes of satin and velvet.

"I never got sick of marionettes as far as I can recall." Mike pauses, then pounds his workbench. "I get sick of the *electric business*!

"I fight with my wife on account of my marionettes."

" 'You and your marionettes,' " he says, mimicking his wife. " 'You and your marionettes.' "

" 'Mary, look. I gotta work on them.' " (Pleading now.)

" 'Ah, there's always work!' " (Scornfully.) "She says, 'You through with the marionettes?'

"There's no such thing as being through with marionettes." His voice rises in exasperation. "There's always something to do."

Each puppet weighs more than one hundred pounds and is only an inch or two shorter than Mike Manteo, but he can still flick them to life with a twitch of his hand. He grew up in a time when strength was the measure of a man, an old-fashioned time when fathers led and families followed. This morning, he has come to teach his grandson.

"*Combate*!" Mike booms in Italian. His deep voice bounces off the walls. The marionettes bash together in a fierce brawl.

"Hit *hard*!"

"Okay!" cries the grandson, struggling to hold on.

"Hard!" Mike vigorously shakes his puppet's head. "See, then I hit you twice."

He bends the marionette from the waist, flips back its cape, raises its sword, and smashes it into the boy's knight. The boy strikes back. Mike stomps his foot, screams, and tosses his doll crashing to the floor like a clumsy waiter. It is a dramatic death.

"Good. Good!" he laughs.

The boy grins. His face looks like a muddy stream in springtime.

Mike worries about a time when all the puppet voices will finally stop and all the tomorrows will be silent. The marionettes are the children of his fantasy. He suspects they may have had their small play. The lives of the younger Manteos now extend far beyond the family workshop. There is no permanent theater for these marionettes.

The old man pulls the puppet from the floor, straightens its cape, and hangs it on a ring in the rafters. He is comfortable with these old things. The wooden heads, pitted with age, scabbed and scarred with battle, are his winter fire. Papa Manteo reaches for the light switch and turns for a final look. The marionettes have been his life. Each has a name, a history. They are pals.

"Good night."

With them, he has created worlds more real than any he ever walked.

EIGHT

I Did It My Way

"... arpeggios by day and their uppercuts by night."
BOB DOTSON

"You Fellas,
Up on the Crosses..."

For some folks, Saturday night in Dallas means Willie and
Waylon and the "Cotton-Eyed Joe." Don Jackson wants to
change all that. Each spring when the New York Metropolitan
Opera comes to town, Jackson sweeps through the city, con-
vincing dozens of cowboys to become moving scenery, opera
extras, so that a chorus of ten will look like a cast of thousands.

Asking a guy in Texas to wear a loincloth in public takes
as much nerve as telling Miss Ellie that J.R. has sold the ranch.
Getting him to take off his boots in the Longhorn Ballroom
for a costume measurement, well, Texans haven't seen that
kind of courage since the Alamo.

"You don't have to sing a note," says Jackson to a cowboy
nursing a long-neck bottle. "You just have to carry a spear."

Jackson is fearless. One time, he went into the red light dis-
trict looking for extras.

"I told them we paid very little," says Jackson, "but one of them said, 'That's okay. We'll make good contacts.' "

In New York, where the opera is a grand tradition, extras attend dozens of rehearsals and learn how to stand with all the seriousness that Luciano Pavarotti reserves for his music. On the road, tradition is taught in twenty minutes. The only rehearsal is just before the actual performance.

There is little room for error. Props are given simple names to help the extras remember. An Egyptian idol that looked vaguely like something to eat prompted this command.

"Hey, you! Grab that pregnant cashew over there!"

Stage directions are doled out like traffic citations.

"You fellas, up on the crosses . . . make a left at the light."

It's about this time that some guys begin to wonder.

"The job pays only five bucks a performance," complains one cowboy. "Nobody said anything about hanging from a cross."

Backstage, Georgio Lamberti is warming up for his lead role in *Aida*. Down the hall, the boys from the Longhorn Ballroom are trying on new duds.

"My tunic is too short," says Jim Bob Jones. "I hope the minister isn't watching."

Franco, the dresser, has tossed out Don Jackson's meticulous measurements. Twenty minutes before curtain, he decided that one size fits all.

Jim Bob lights a cigarette and leans against the wall.

"You just have to take it, I guess. Egyptian stuff, ugh!"

It's a long way from the Longhorn Ballroom to backstage with the Met. The closest Jim Bob had come to an audience before tonight was catching passes on a football field. But he was soon to find that the game plan is the same.

"All right, boys!" cries the stage director. "Line up!"

Jim Bob and four others pick up the "pregnant cashew."

"Ouch!"

"What's the matter?"

"This sucker won't go through!" Jim Bob is whispering now. "It's hung up."

"Where?" hisses the stage manager.

"On the curtain."

The orchestra roars. Spotlights spear the stage. The guys on the crosses groan heavily.

"Move it back."

"Hurry, boys. Hurry."

"Cashew! Where's Cashew?"

"Here, sir . . . I reckon," says Jim Bob.

"Where?"

"In the curtain."

"Oh, G——."

"Pull him out."

A half dozen hands swirl around the cashew. On stage, the

Hoisting the pregnant cashew

guys carrying the crosses circle a second time. The cowboys who are hanging groan a little louder.

"Turn. Tug. Tug."

Jim Bob reaches and yanks with all his might, gathering the cashew to his side. The prop pops free.

"Miller time!" chuckles Jim Bob, as he stumbles into the spotlight. He is the only "slave" smiling.

"It's just like football," he says later. "That opera . . . it's just a game of inches."

It's the Pits

The Texas spiny lizard knows something about survival. He is very difficult to find. Almost impossible to capture. That's why scientists have chased it for years. They believe that studying the spiny lizard will help them save other animals.

There are some time-honored methods for nabbing the tiny critters, providing you can find one. Some scientists use a short noose on a long pole. Others try a quick lunge from the lizard's blind side. Neither method works too well.

Enter Dr. Lloyd Fitzpatrick. He has found a better way. Dr. Fitzpatrick stalks the wily lizard with . . . a blow gun. He hardly ever misses, even more amazing when you consider his ammunition—pimento-stuffed olives.

"Well, we use the pimento-stuffed olives instead of the ones with the pits," says Dr. Fitzpatrick, "because they are softer and they don't damage the lizard as much. A pitted olive would kill the little thing."

He drops another olive into his blowpipe.

"Also, we use the pimento because it acts like a tracer. If we shoot over the lizard's head, the pimento sticks to the tree, and we can change our trajectory accordingly."

"What caliber olive do you use?" I ask.

Dr. Fitzpatrick looks up into a tree. Spots a lizard.

"I think it's a fifty-nine caliber."

POW!

"Kind of a dumdum," I say.

"Yeah," says Dr. Fitzpatrick, "a real dumb-dumb."

A tiny lizard falls into an assistant's hand.

"Are there any occupational hazards?" I ask.

"Well," says Dr. Fitzpatrick, "there is one that has been known to get a hunter, once in a while. If you try to hit a lizard at some distance, you need to take a big breath of air. And sometimes you inhale the olive. That's a real drag," he laughs.

Despite its drawbacks, the olive has revolutionized spiny lizard research. Dr. Fitzpatrick now has plenty of specimens to study in his biology lab, and someday his spiny lizards may help save other animals. In the meantime, the research has its rewards.

"What we try to do," says Dr. Fitzpatrick, "is recycle the olives. My assistants and I have, over the years, become quite proficient and efficient in using the olives, so we have some left for drinks at the end of the day."

Junk Food Critic

DALLAS, TEXAS
(1981)

What can I say about George Toomer? Let me first give you an insight into what George considers funny. Toomer lives in Dallas. A few years back, "bored and disgusted with the whole Kennedy assassination pageantry," he paid a visit to the Texas School Book Depository where John F. Kennedy was killed. He strolled casually atop the famous grassy knoll where conspiracy buffs insist a second gunman stood; then George surreptitiously scattered a pocketful of empty rifle shells for tourists to find in an attempt to establish the "fifteen gun theory."

That has nothing to do with the rest of this story, but I thought it would brighten your day.

George Toomer is a food critic for "D" magazine ("D" for Dallas.) Most food critics get the benefit of dining in some fine restaurants. Not George. He is a self-proclaimed "junk food centurion," a "confectionary kamikaze," a man who reviews the food that most of us eat.

"I'd be going to lunch with some fellow critics, and they'd say, 'Let's go to Mercelles.' And I'd go, 'Oh, no, I'm in a hurry; let's just go eat at Wendy's.' And they'd put me down. I mean, they would make such a thing about eating a Wendy's burger that I'd feel so guilty. I like them. Everybody I know likes them. So I suddenly started realizing that there was a far greater service I could do than chart the course of next year's truffles."

Obviously, George Toomer is not part of the granola-for-lunch bunch. He's a food critic who looks like Orson Welles but prefers to eat like Popeye's pal, Wimpy.

"I love hamburgers!" he says, "but some places that serve 'em are terrible! I think they apply their meat with a caulking gun."

We are sitting (where else?) in Wendy's. He eyes a plate stacked high with "research."

"It's a tough job, but—GULP!" (One hamburger gone)— "Somebody's gotta review 'em."

George sports a 280-pound résumé to prove his dedication to his work.

"Sure, I'm fat," says Toomer, "but I don't just sit around snarfing hamburgers all day."

He reviews all kinds of junk food.

"When you get right down to it, gourmet cooking is not really very important. Ask yourself how many people have eaten a soufflé? Gourmet cooking is in the same category as designer label jeans."

Toomer got hooked on junk food as a boy. His mother once found him fondling a bottle of Bosco and a half-empty case of My-T-Fine pudding.

After lunch, he takes me to a grocery store and starts grabbing boxes.

"Why do they call it junk food?" he wails. "I think the

name is just a plot of the healthier-than-thou crowd. Looky here. There's a whole social structure that has been built up on what kind of chips and snacks you have at your party. If you're a health nut, you always go for something that everyone kind of hates. But your choice implies that *you* really kind of like it."

Toomer clutches a box of crackers.

"People really like *these*. But you say to yourself, 'Look, everybody's going to be weight conscious or nutrition conscious. So I'll get this cracker called Vegetable Thins.' I mean, *Vegetable Thins*!" Toomer shouts, holding the box between two fingers like a dirty diaper. "Look, there's a guilt-free chip. You lay that out at your party and people say, 'He's suffering right along with us.'"

Toomer stops his cart in front of a freezer compartment, pulls out a frozen pizza, and taps it on his head.

"Some pizza tastes like a giant soda cracker with a big red stain on it. They have little pepperonis that look like they're cut out of garden hose. This pizza tastes like a sock. I do comparative studies. I try to tell people which is best."

Later, at his apartment, I observe that he doesn't need much of a kitchen for gourmet du junk.

"No, actually you just need one famous utensil," says Toomer, "a pair of tongs to lift the boiling pouches out of the pot. I've got that down to a science. I can hold that little rascal with tongs, take a steak knife, cut off the top of the pouch, pour it over rice, put the pouch in the trash, and *never* touch my hands to anything."

George urges his readers to come out of the closet and eat Twinkies in the sunshine.

"All you need to wash away the guilt," he says, "is a touch of class."

We are sitting on his back porch, finishing our supper. There are flowers on the table. The contents of aluminum cans have been transferred to good china. George has chosen well. Few people could tell without looking through his trash that our

Dinner with the junk food critic

meal was all fast food. I pour the wine, he passes the dessert. Surely, it is time for reflection.

"Does a Twinkie get better with age?" I ask.

George drops his head and glances up from under an arched eyebrow. He is savoring his thoughts like a good sauce.

"You should serve no Twinkie before its time."

Arpeggios and Uppercuts

DALLAS, TEXAS
(1981)

All that nonsense about the weaker sex was thought up by adults. Remember who was the toughest kid at the playground? Yeah, a girl. Always a girl. A kid by the name of Martha Heffelfinger gave me a lesson in equal rights long before the women's movement—equal rights, equal lefts punched my lights out. Imagine if she'd had some training.

"I think you've got him on the ropes now!" cries the pudgy little man. "Next time, hit him faster and harder."

The small girl shuffles across the canvas, her head a blur of pigtails and sweat.

"Punch him! Jab him, Lori. Stick him!"

The little girl closes in on her opponent and disappears in his shadow.

POP! POP! POP!

The old gym is dark. The small pudgy man leans closer to see. There is only the shadow and the noise.

POP! POP! POP!

"Good, Lori, keep it up."

Lori Marroquin looks least likely to follow in Martha Heffelfinger's footsteps. She is short for her eight years.

POW!

Lori can flatten a boy nearly twice her size.

She gets help from a most unusual source. The little man slipping through the ropes is her piano teacher. He is also her boxing coach.

By day, Doyle Weaver is as mild-mannered as Clark Kent. By night, he punches more than arpeggios. Weaver is a quiet Walter Mitty who dreams of making boxers out of his piano students. He has taught music all of his life, but his hero is Joe Louis.

"Louis was dangerous every minute," says Weaver. "He was the most exciting fighter I think I've ever known."

"You have to admit," I say, "piano playing and boxing are a strange combination."

"Yes," he admits, helping a boy up from the mat, "but they both require confidence and coordination."

Weaver is the founder and coach of the oldest girls' boxing team in America. Kids four to sixteen practice their arpeggios by day and their uppercuts by night.

Lisa Warren has had fifty fights. She has never lost.

Bobbye Lynne Bowen, now an instructor, was so confident she battled successfully in twenty-five bouts—with braces on her teeth.

Naturally, parents are a bit reluctant at first. But there has never been a broken bone, and rarely even a black eye. Lori's folks have become fans.

"Are you going to tell the boys who come calling for dates about Lori's hobby?" I ask.

"No," laughs Mrs. Marroquin, "I'm going to let them find out for themselves."

Weaver's girls do well because they train hard. He tackles

practice as he would a polonaise. The secret, Doyle says, is to start them young. Girls develop more quickly than boys.

I already knew that.

"Punch me right here," says Weaver. "Let's see if it hurts." He is taunting a four-year-old rookie with blonde pigtails and big red boxing gloves.

WHACK!

"Goodness! It does hurt!"

Weaver's nose begins to look like the one on Santa's lead reindeer.

Girls do have an advantage . . . a guy can get a little over confident.

Lady Eye

DELRAY BEACH, FLORIDA
(1982)

Authorities in south Florida are puzzling over a case known hereabouts as the "great Trojan caper." A guy delivered a big crate to a bank vault for safekeeping. There should have been a statue inside. Instead, there was a crook in the crate, a man with enough food, water, and tools to make it through the weekend and rob the bank. He might have made it, if it hadn't been for a guard who, no doubt, knew his classics.

There was some question as to who was the brains behind that box burglary. So folks hired a very special private eye to find out. Virginia Snyder looks like the kind of little old lady Boy Scouts fight over to help across the street. At retirement age, Virginia opened her own detective agency. With no prior police training, she became one of only two women in Florida to get a class A investigator's license.

The cases she handles are none too dainty—murders,

Virginia Snyder in disguise

muggings, drug addiction. Informants trust her because she doggedly pursues facts wherever they take her.

She keeps a trunk full of disguises for safety.

"The whole point is to blend into the environment," she says, "to do whatever you're doing so naturally that people just give you a passing glance."

Her best cover is her grandmotherly appearance—now a bird watcher, now a bag lady waiting for a bus. On one stakeout in front of a hotel, she sat on the passenger side of her car.

"Just a wife," she says, "apparently waiting for her husband."

When a policeman asked her what she was doing . . .

"I put on my righteous indignation act," says Virginia, "and told the officer, 'I'm waiting for that no-good husband of mine. I'll leave if you want me to. But when he comes out of there, I don't care if it takes all night, I'm going to catch him!' "

The policeman let her stay.

"Snoopy calling Red Baron. Snoopy calling Red Baron."

Virginia is tailing a suspect, snapping at the switch on her CB radio. "The white car coming towards you. Watch it as it goes by. See if it's a man or a woman driving."

"It's a man," answers her husband, hiding in a panel truck, looking through a peephole.

"Ten-four," says Virginia.

I ask her, "Don't you sometimes just say, 'I ought to be out there with the sand between my toes, or playing golf along with the other folks who come down to Florida?' "

"I can't think of anything more boring," she replies, making a quick left to keep the suspect in sight. "Can you imagine, all day long with *nothing* to do? Think of the human potential that we have just in Florida. All of these retirees with education, background, experience, brains, capabilities, talents, are out on the golf courses, out on the beaches. Think of the millions that are out there. Those people should be doing something."

Well, Virginia Snyder looks at retirement a bit differently than most.

"But, you see," she grins, "I always wanted to be something special when I grew up."

"What was that?" I ask.

"Happy!" she said.

"Snoopy to Red Baron. Snoopy to Red Baron."

"Go ahead."

"Don't wait dinner. I've spotted him."

NINE

Names We Never Knew

"*...a heritage of the common man*"
BOB DOTSON

And He Was
Signing It for Them

"America was built by just folks," said Charles Banks Wilson, staring out the window of his artist's studio. Behind him were huge images of cowboys and Indians, trappers and pioneers—four paint-spattered murals, twenty-seven-foot tall, propped above the relics of their creation. Pencil sketches and clay figures lay scattered about. Dozens of history books were stacked on tables. Five years earlier, Wilson had set out to paint the world's largest textbook—a heritage for the common man.

"I felt I owed it to that guy who dug the water well, or that surveyor with the interesting story," he said, pointing to the figures before him, "to show them just as well as I could."

Wilson turned and walked through the single shaft of light that came through his east window. He crossed the room, which was big and dark and boomy, then pulled himself up on a wooden scaffold and climbed forty feet above the concrete floor.

"In most written history, they tell you who, what, when, where, and how," said Wilson, as he picked up a palette and worked with a fine brush. "They almost never tell you what things looked like."

He dabbed paint on a small cabin.

"If you notice," said Wilson, "in that little shack is a black-smith. A blacksmith is a black man, which very few people realize. Over in Europe, the man who did that kind of work was called a 'smithy' or 'smitty.' But when folks came over here, black men prepared the metal products in many trading posts, so, naturally, they were called blacksmiths."

Wilson shifted his brush to the figure of a massive Indian wrapped in fur pelts.

"The Osage Indians were lovers of dogs," he continued after a stroke or two. "In my research I found that Osages wore buffalo robes around their waist and their legs, even in the summertime. I asked, why? Well, they wore those buffalo robes, not to protect them from the weather, but to protect them from the dogs who didn't have enough to eat. The dogs would eat their leggings off! I found accounts where overnight the dogs would eat up a whole teepee."

"Why'd they keep the dogs?" I asked.

Wilson touched his moustache. "Well," he said matter-of-factly, "they liked dogs."

The Oklahoma legislature commissioned Wilson to paint this visual textbook. The work was to hang under the dome at the state capitol. For two years, there was not a stroke on canvas. Wilson searched dusty archives and drifted back roads looking for descriptions.

"I wanted people who stood before my murals to say, 'Those folks looked just like that.' " he said.

There are no monuments to the common man, but there are traces in the weeds of time. Later that day, we took a small boat and went searching.

"When you cross that bridge and look to the right, you'll

see the falls of the Verdigris River," said Wilson as we floated past shadows and sun. "To the left, on that high knoll is the location of Chouteau's fort. He was an old French trader.

"There were nine thousand Indians at his fort. Three thousand trappers and something like five thousand traders. Each spring, they built flatboats to carry their pelts down to New Orleans. There weren't any pensions or that sort of thing in those days. So, the benefits, the fringe benefits, were so much whiskey a week. And I understand that Sam Houston was probably the biggest whiskey dealer that ever came up the Verdigris. I'm not taking away from the man's fame, but he was criticized by the other traders because he always had more whiskey and could get more flatboat builders."

We nosed our boat ashore and stepped into the forest.

"Those flatboats," said Wilson, "were built out of exotic woods—walnut, pecan—anything that was available. They were filled with buffalo robes and deer hides for shipment to New Orleans and then on to Europe. Of course, once they got the stuff to New Orleans, they had an empty flatboat and they couldn't bring it back up the river. The river doesn't run that way. So they'd sell the wood right there. This wood would be sold to a French wood-carver in New Orleans, and he would turn it into a fine piece of French furniture. It would stay around New Orleans for a couple of hundred years, and then someone from out West, who was down there visiting the Mardi Gras, would see this beautiful piece and bring it back up the Verdigris as an antique."

The wind blew the tall grass between the trees, and the water birds rose toward the bridge screaming at passing cars. We shoved our boat back into the river.

"I was afraid of this job," said Wilson, "because I knew what was going to happen, and I doubted that I was really capable of doing what was expected."

He watched the birds for a moment.

"I went through h__. I couldn't sleep at night. I had nightmares. I knew what was coming! I knew how I was going to have to give up everything else I was doing."

Perhaps it would have been easier simply to paint a wrought-iron dream against a stained glass sky. Perhaps there was no need for years of research and late night wandering. But Charles Banks Wilson was working for the people who never had time to own a dream. And he was signing it for them.

Several months later, Wilson called to say that the job was finished. I went by to see him. The street lights had just come on outside his studio window. We approached the huge figures through the shadows, our footsteps echoing off the walls.

"Late one evening, a few weeks before the murals were completed," said Wilson, "I sensed that something was wrong."

He got dressed and went to his workshop. The door to his office was open!

Wilson bounded up the stairs. In the cavernous darkness of his studio, a figure was outlined in the night. Fumbling for a light, Wilson recognized the man—Joe Noel, a roofer who had posed for the mural, one of the last of the pure-blood Choctaws.

"You know, Charlie," said Noel, spinning to face him. "I just had to come back and take a look."

The man stood silently beneath his massive image.

"You know, the Choctaws are really happy that I'm up there," said Noel at last.

He straightened his hat and walked to the stairs.

"Good night, Charlie."

The next morning, Wilson was back—touching up Joe Noel's figure.

CHRISTIAN HERALD ASSOCIATION AND ITS MINISTRIES

CHRISTIAN HERALD ASSOCIATION, founded in 1878, publishes The Christian Herald Magazine, one of the leading interdenominational religious monthlies in America. Through its wide circulation, it brings inspiring articles and the latest news of religious developments to many families. From the magazine's pages came the initiative for CHRISTIAN HERALD CHILDREN and THE BOWERY MISSION, two individually supported not-for-profit corporations.

CHRISTIAN HERALD CHILDREN, established in 1894, is the name for a unique and dynamic ministry to disadvantaged children, offering hope and opportunities which would not otherwise be available for reasons of poverty and neglect. The goal is to develop each child's potential and to demonstrate Christian compassion and understanding to children in need.

Mont Lawn is a permanent camp located in Bushkill, Pennsylvania. It is the focal point of a ministry which provides a healthful "vacation with a purpose" to children who without it would be confined to the streets of the city. Up to 1000 children between the age of 7 and 11 come to Mont Lawn each year.

Christian Herald Children maintains year-round contact with children by means of a *City Youth Ministry.* Central to its philosophy is the belief that only through sustained relationships and demonstrated concern can individual lives be truly enriched. Special emphasis is on individual guidance, spiritual and family counseling and tutoring. This follow-up ministry to inner-city children culminates for many in financial assistance toward higher education and career counseling.

THE BOWERY MISSION, located at 227 Bowery, New York City, has since 1879 been reaching out to the lost men on the Bowery, offering them what could be their last chance to rebuild their lives. Every man is fed, clothed and ministered to. Countless numbers have entered the 90-day residential rehabilitation program at the Bowery Mission. A concentrated ministry of counseling, medical care, nutrition therapy, Bible study and Gospel services awakens a man to spiritual renewal within himself.

These ministries are supported solely by the voluntary contributions of individuals and by legacies and bequests. Contributions are tax deductible. Checks should be made out either to CHRISTIAN HERALD CHILDREN or to THE BOWERY MISSION.

Administrative Office: 40 Overlook Drive, Chappaqua, New York 10514
Telephone: (914) 769-9000

BOB DOTSON began his work for NBC News as a reporter at WKYC-TV, the NBC affiliate in Cleveland. He has been with the "Today" show since December 1978 and now also contributes stories to the NBC "Nightly News with Tom Brokaw."

Dotson was born in St. Louis, Missouri, received a Bachelor of Science degree in journalism and political science from Kansas University and a Master of Science in television from Syracuse University. He has been based in Atlanta since 1979.

During his journalism career Dotson has received more than thirty-five awards, including a CLARION award from Women in Communications, an Emmy Award, a DuPont-Columbia Award, and the Robert F. Kennedy Award for Outstanding Television Program of 1974.

Dotson and his wife, the former Linda Puckett, have a daughter, Amy.